# *Classic*
# SCOOTERS
## 1945–1970

## Other Titles in the Crowood MotoClassics Series

# *Classic* SCOOTERS
# 1945–1970

**Mick Walker**

THE CROWOOD PRESS

First published in 2008 by
The Crowood Press Ltd
Ramsbury, Marlborough
Wiltshire SN8 2HR

**www.crowood.com**

**British Library Cataloguing-in-Publication Data**
A catalogue record for this book is available from the
British Library.

ISBN 978 1 86126 967 6

**Acknowledgements**
Thanks to Shaun Ackroyd, Brian Crook, Michael
Dregni, Derek Farrar, Matthew Vale, Mike Webster,
Eddie Weeks, Jez Wensor of Lincs Lambrettas, members
of The Vintage Motor Scooter Club, and Pook's Motor
Bookshop.

Typeset by Phoenix Typesetting, Auldgirth,
Dumfriesshire.

Printed and bound in Singapore by Craft Print
International Ltd

# Contents

# Preface

Although I had begun my riding career on scooters rather than motor cycles, the initial idea for this book came from the publishers rather than me. Indeed, my first impression of the project was that I wasn't too keen. However, once I began researching and writing this all changed as I realized just what a fascinating subject it was, and before long I was filled with genuine enthusiasm. These small vehicles were produced in such a wide range of types, engine sizes, and in so many countries, that the more I got into the task the more interesting it became. Another surprise was the sheer breadth of technical innovation and engineering skills shown by the various designers and engineers, to say nothing of the many firms, both large and small, who jumped on the scooter bandwagon. During the period covered by this book, there were well over two hundred manufacturers throughout western Europe, behind the Iron Curtain, in the USA and Japan.

I hope that you will get as much pleasure from reading this book as I have had in writing it.

Mick Walker
Wisbech, Cambridgeshire
June 2007

# 1   Origins and Cult

## Origins

The first scooters appeared after the Great War of 1914–18. They came about due to the public's need for inexpensive personal transport. And although these early attempts – largely from manufacturers in the USA, Great Britain and Germany – were on the whole unsuccessful from a sales point of view, they did spawn far greater interest and ultimately widespread use of scooters during the period covered by this book.

Long before the rush to build scooters from 1945–70 there was what could be called the 'origins' period. The very first machines that could be truly defined as scooters were the American Motoped and Autoped machines of 1915–16, but it was from 1919 onwards that

*First patented in the USA on 19 May 1915, the 155cc Autoped was subsequently built under licence in both Great Britain and Germany. Also in the frame is a James motorcycle, circa early 1950s.*

*Kingsbury were an aircraft company based in Croydon, Surrey. From 1919 until 1923 they built this very basic scooter, powered by a 254cc two-stroke engine.*

the concept really began in earnest, and the vast majority of the early scooters were built between this time and 1945.

**Aviation Interest**

Although the First and Second World Wars had led to catastrophic suffering and loss of life, vast strides were made during both conflicts in many areas of technical development. Aircraft manufacturers in Italy, Germany and Japan, which had often made the greatest advances in technology, were the very ones who in the aftermath of the conflicts turned to the production of powered two-wheelers, in particular scooters.

Great Britain was also amongst the first to produce these machines, manufacturers including the All British (Engine) Company (ABC), Roe, and Gloucester Aircraft.

**ABC**

The All British (Engine) Company (ABC) was connected with Sopwith, the aero engine manufacturer that had built the famous Camel fighter of World War I and, from 1912, motor cycles. ABC produced scooters from 1920–21. In 1919 Granville Bradshaw created the ABC Skootamota, which went on sale in 1920. At first this had a 147cc inlet-over-exhaust single-cylinder engine; later this

*The German DKW Lamos of 1924 employed a 142cc two-stroke engine and, although a poor seller, it had many interesting features, notably front and rear suspension – the latter by a long swinging arm with twin telescopic legs.*

*Designed by Granville Bradshaw, the ABC Skootamota was manufactured in conjunction with the Surrey-based Sopwith Aviation Company.*

*Rear-mounted Skootamota engine with massive outside flywheel.*

was supplemented by a 110cc overhead-valve power unit.

## Roe

A V Roe was one of Great Britain's premier aviation names. As early as 1905 he had taken an interest in powered two-wheelers, proposing a motor cycle with much more comprehensive mudguarding, and he later constructed a complete machine using a Douglas engine. Then, in 1922, Roe designed and built the Avro Mobile, which had low seating, full enclosure and small wheels, powered by a 349cc Barr & Stroud engine. This interesting scooter had a frame constructed

from sheet steel, whilst other notable features included hub-centre steering and 12in disc wheels.

## Gloucester Aircraft Company

The Unibus scooter, which was manufactured by the Gloucester Aircraft Company and built from 1920–22, could well have passed for a 1950s design. Created by Harold Boultbee, it had, for its day, an ultra-modern style, with a flat floor behind a curvaceous front wind-shield, the body having a channel-section frame with leaf-spring suspension at front and rear. The 269cc two-stroke engine was positioned just aft of the steering column and hidden from view behind the apron. Advanced as it was, the Unibus was expensive and attracted only limited sales, but it was an early sign of what lay ahead.

## Soon Gone

However, as the 1920s unfolded, the early scooters' success rapidly declined in both Europe and the USA. According to arch-scooter enthusiast Michael Dregni it 'was just a passing fancy in the Roaring Twenties, going the way of the Charleston and steam-powered automobiles. The first wave of scooters died by the side of the road as quickly as it was born.'

## A Second Wave

The second scooter boom began in Oakland, California, during the mid-1930s in the small workshop of E. Foster Salsbury and the engineer Austin Elmore. As Michael Dregni noted, 'In 1935, Salsbury had seen the great feminist and aviator Amelia Earhart frolic around the Lockheed airport at Burbank on a left-over Motoped Scooter.' And as Salsbury himself said when interviewed in 1992, 'It got me starting thinking about building a real scooter'. As detailed in Chapter 6, Elmore constructed the first machine, the prototype Motor Glide, in late 1935, and it made its public bow early the following year. Again, according to Michael Dregni, 'The design of Salsbury and Elmore's 1936 Motor Glide spread like a contagious disease: Powell, Moto-Scoot, Cushman, Rock-Ola, and many others were offering their own scooters in the Motor Glide mode by the end of 1936.'

The Salsbury Motor Glide defined the five requirements for a motor scooter that set the style for all scooters that were to follow: a small motor placed next to or just in front of the rear wheel; a step-through chassis; bodywork to protect the rider from road spray and engine grime; small wheels; and an automatic trans-

*Unlike the Skootamota, the Autoglider had its 269cc Villiers two-stroke engine mounted over the front wheel. Designed by Charles R Townsend, the prototype was constructed in 1919. The version shown here dates from 1921 with a 292cc Union engine and horizontal fuel tank (the earlier model's tank was vertical).*

mission/clutch package. All other scooters that came after the Motor Glide had at least three of these five attributes.

Then came the Second World War and the second scooter wave largely disappeared as the conflict unfolded, certainly as far as the civilian market was concerned.

## The War Scooter

And so came about what I have called 'the war scooter'. This was largely intended for use by airborne forces, who needed a compact, basic form of motorized transport, often behind enemy lines, examples of these being the American Cushman 244cc, the Italian *Volu grafo Aermoto* 125cc and the British Welbike 98cc.

The American design employed a single-cylinder four-stroke engine, with side-valves, fan-cooling and magneto, and was a much larger machine than the two diminutive European designs, both of which used simple air-cooled two-stroke power units.

No less a man than Enrico Piaggio was to

*Touring was also a major part of the scooterist's life. This German NSU Prima not only has a Bambini sidecar fitted, but is kitted out with 1950s period tartan panniers, bags and even a spare wheel cover.*

comment later that the *Volugrafo Aermoto* had planted the seed of a post-war scooter in his mind.

## The Post-War Miracle

Piaggio must take a large part of the credit for helping to create this event with their legendary Vespa brand. Piaggio was soon joined by fellow Italian industrial giant Innocenti and its Lambretta, and it was the Italians who sparked off the vast scooter sales boom that lasted from the late 1940s until well into the 1960s. This boom eventually spread to the rest of Europe, Japan and the USA. Just how this was achieved and by whom is charted in Chapters 2–8.

Soon, scooters were not only being used as a basic form of transportation, but also, due to the arrival of larger, more powerful models, touring and many forms of competition including rallying, trials, scooter-cross, road racing and even record-breaking. The age of the scooter had arrived!

## The Scooter Culture

The Vespa was a brilliant concept – a combination of just what the customer wanted. This formula of style and reliability, economy and technical innovation, made it a winner half a century ago – and the reason why it is still in production today.

The Vespa, together with the Lambretta, was largely instrumental in giving the scooter cult status. The scooter did a magnificent job of bringing people together, spreading ideas and cultures and generally promoting a sense of well-being – all at a bargain basement price. And unlike the motor cycle, which was largely seen as a man's machine, the scooter was equally loved by both sexes with its mixture of mobility, style and affordability. And so the scooter culture grew. As the 1950s blossomed, the scooter gained more and more devotees.

*The Vespa Club*

**OF BRITAIN . . .**

*welcomes you to the ever-increasing family of Vespa Owners.*

*A family that began in Italy and multiplied amazingly through France and is now firmly established in Britain—a swarming, widely scattered and an extremely friendly family.*

*A Vespa Club of Britain brochure, circa mid-1950s. Club life was a big part of the scooter scene during that decade.*

*A group of Lambretta Club Italia members prove their skill and the robustness of their machines!*

*A British Douglas-Vespa accessory catalogue, listing hundreds of items including mirrors, wheel discs, front bumpers, floormats windscreens, dual seats and much more.*

The fifties had been the age of the film star, and the scooter – the Vespa in particular – was often to be seen in the big movies of the day. The arrival of the Swinging Sixties brought with it the age of the pop star, and again the scooter embraced this new trend.

Summing up, scooter buff Mike Webster says:

> If 'classic' simply meant quantity, then this book would be full of Lambrettas and Vespas. The truth is that a number of largely unknown, low-volume scooters were well-engineered, high-quality, innovative machines … the variety of engineering solutions is testimony to individualistic engineers and talented designers far removed from the computer-aided design of the virtually identical offerings of today.

## Clubs

The popularity of scooters soon led to a host of clubs being formed world-wide. Typical was the Vespa Club of Great Britain. The origins of this organization can be traced to May 1952 when a railway engineer who had acquired one of the then recently introduced Douglas Vespa machines felt that there was a need in the north-west of London for an owners' club. He canvassed for support, the result being the formation of the North-West London Vespa Club – the first such club in Great Britain. This small start eventually led to the formation of

no fewer than 120 local clubs by mid-1959, when the national membership stood at 4,000. And by the end of the 1950s, every country in western Europe, with the exception of Norway, had its own Vespa national organization, overseen by the Vespa Club of Europe.

This meant that there were opportunities to compete in events in continental Europe, including the Eurovespa Rally. In Barcelona in

*Crystal Palace Scooter Training School, London, in the late 1950s.*

*Lambretta LD150 owner Mrs M J Steele, after being voted Miss Scooter Girl at the 1958 World Scooter Rally in the Isle of Man. The machine is typical of the time, with white wall tyres and various chrome-plated extras.*

1957, the British team won the award for formation riding. Then in 1958, British Vespa riders, attired in 'City of London' gents' outfits, including bowler hats and rolled umbrellas, carried off the award for the best national dress.

## Competitions

As described in more detail in Chapter 9, scooter sport was very much a part of the 1950s and 1960s scene, the Isle of Man scooter events being the stuff of legends with all sorts of competitions including time trials, sand racing, hill climbing, concours and much more. In earlier years there were even 24-hour marathons.

There were also the long-distance road events, the famous Esso Scoot to Scotland (London to Edinburgh) being just one such popular gathering.

## The Mods

The Mods (and Rockers) were very much part of the 1960s youth culture in Great Britain. As everyone knows, the Mods rode scooters; the Rockers, motor cycles.

Whereas Rockers had BSA Gold Stars, Triumph Bonnevilles and the like, the Mods rode Lambrettas and Vespas. And from around 1960, they transformed their machines – lashings of chrome plate, extra lights, spare wheels, countless mirrors and even handlebar tassels, to stripped-down creations whose frames were bereft of almost any bodywork whatsoever. Noisy sports silencers were mandatory, and, instead of outright performance, the Mod's aspiration was to corner his machine with the footboards raising sparks against the tarmac.

Rivalry between Mods and Rockers ran high, with the first well-publicized troubles coming in the summer of 1964 when the two groups converged for a Bank Holiday 'battle' on the beaches of Brighton – in what had begun as an innocent Lambretta-sponsored club event. This confrontation was seized upon by the media and exaggerated to such a degree that anyone not actually there would have imagined that World War Three had broken out!

During the mid-late 1960s, scarcely a summer weekend seemed to pass without reports of the Mod-Rocker clashes on the seafronts of not just Brighton, but several other towns including Southend and Great Yarmouth – the news media highlighting

*A BSA 175 Sunbeam and Triumph 250 Tigress at John O'Groats Hotel during an Auto Cycle Union-observed demonstration in 1960.*

terrified locals, irate shopkeepers and over-stretched police services.

Today, there are still scooter rallies in Great Yarmouth and the annual 'Rockers Reunion' in Brighton. However, the 'battles' of the past are long since over and all but forgotten now. On both sides, the aggressive youth culture of four decades ago has given way to moderate,

and doubtless sometimes nostalgic, middle age.

But the memories, good and bad, of bygone scooter days, have only helped maintain and actually fuel the cult of the scooter. This, combined with the growing appreciation of just what the scooter did to alter our very culture, has ensured this humble machine a special place in history.

# 2 Italy and Spain

## The Italians Lead The Way

As previously described, it was the Italians who reinvented the scooter in the years following the end of the Second World War. Many major engineering firms lay idle, having lost the military contracts that they had received in earlier years, and needed something to replace them. This, and the desire to get the country mobile again, led the two industrial giants, Piaggio and Innocenti, to produce the Vespa and Lambretta scooters, respectively. Many other Italian scooter builders followed their lead.

Enrico Piaggio was later to admit that his particular inspiration had been the tiny

*The Vespa made its first public bow at the Milan Spring Fair of 1946.*

Aermoto, a lightweight military parachute scooter with dual front and rear wheels and a low-set frame similar to the British Welbike. Built by *Societá Volugrafo* of Turin, the Aermoto was powered by a single-cylinder 125cc two-stroke engine with a two-speed gearbox and pressed steel wheels, these split rims becoming a notable feature of the majority of post-war scooters.

## Vespa – The Background

*Societiá Anonima Piaggio* had been founded back in 1884 by Rinaldo Piaggio in Genoa, making woodworking machinery for the local shipbuilding industry. In 1901 it turned to railway rolling stock and in 1915 moved into aviation. Then in 1924 a car manufacturing plant was acquired in Pontedasa. By the time Rinaldo Piaggio died in 1938 – leaving the company to his sons Enrico and Armando – the Piaggio empire was already vast, with several production facilities and a work force of 10,000.

During the war Piaggio built numerous aircraft engine types and Italy's only long-range, four-engined heavy bomber, the P108.

But by 1944, following several heavy bombing raids by the Allies, all that was left of the Piaggio plants were ruined buildings and a workforce trustfully awaiting their next meal ticket; even the remaining machine tools had been confiscated by the Germans! And so Enrico Piaggio, knowing he could no longer rely on aviation for the future of his company, decided to abandon this industrial avenue and

*A feature of the Vespa design was the compact nature of the engine, transmission and rear wheel assemblies, designed very much as a single unit.*

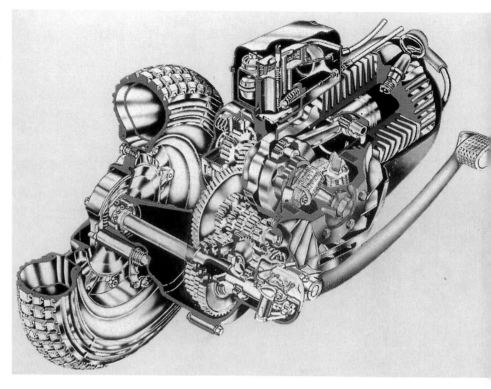

begin a new one that was based upon a cheap and practical means of personal transportation, and would help get his beloved Italy moving again after the horrors of the Second World War. This initial project was entrusted to a pair of engineers, Renzo Spolti and Vittorio Casini.

### The Original Machine

The first prototype of the Piaggio scooter was coded MP5, but was soon nicknamed the *Paperino* (small duck) – after Walt Disney's cartoon character, Donald Duck.

This first attempt was powered by a German Sachs single-cylinder two-stroke engine and featured direct drive (no gearbox), a tunnel-frame manufactured of pressed sheet steel with a centrally mounted engine. Both the engine and frame were totally enclosed within comprehensive bodywork. And unlike what followed, the bodywork ran almost level with the seat base, forward towards the middle of the rider's leg shields, the latter running down-wards from the steering head. This created a negative feature that would have made the scooter unpopular with Piaggio's potential female customers as straddling the scooter by the fairer sex would have been difficult, to say the least!

This, together with certain other details, not the least of which was the sheer bulk of the machine, prompted Enrico Piaggio to axe the design and commission another designer to come up with something different.

In fact Piaggio themselves were later to admit, 'the first motor scooter [the *Paperino*] was a horrible looking thing, and people ridiculed us to our faces'.

### Enter Corradino D'Ascanio

Enrico Piaggio set Corradino D'Ascanio, a respected designer of aircraft and helicopters, to transfer his engineering experience into an entirely new field. The result was to be absolutely stunning and at the same time

19

revolutionary. Not just this, but it was to stand the test of time better than probably any other motor transport vehicle.

D'Ascanio's creation (coded MP6), benefited from the designer's wide aeronautical experience.

When interviewed by an Italian magazine of the period he gave an insight into his priorities when considering the project:

*From 1963 you could even buy a 50cc Vespa.*

Having witnessed motorcyclists stranded at the side of the road many times with a punctured tyre, I decided that one of the most important things to solve was that a flat should no longer be a large problem just like it wasn't for automobiles. Another problem to resolve was that of simplifying the steering, especially in city driving. To help this, the control of gear changing was positioned on the handlebars for easy changing without abandoning manoeuvrability, making its use intuitive for the novice. Another large inconvenience with traditional motor cycles was oil spraying on clothes, so I thought of moving the engine far from the 'pilot', covering it with a fairing, and abolishing the open chain with a cover placing the wheel right next to the gearbox.

Some solutions came from aeronautical technology, with which Piaggio was obviously familiar, such as the rear tubular wheel holder that was borrowed directly from the undercarriage of aircraft. The single shell frame surpassed even the most modern automobile design, since the stamped bodywork of strengthened steel was a rarity. The new machine was also easy to straddle, being reminiscent of a woman's bicycle.

### The Vespa Is Born

Strangely, the biggest problem Piaggio faced when producing its Vespa scooter was its name. At the time, the Piaggio works were switching their production lines from wartime aviation production to an innovative peacetime venture with its new scooter, which was to be called the *Vespa* (wasp). MV Agusta, another former aviation giant, was also switching from aviation to motor cycles, and its first motor cycle had the name Vespa, too. However, Piaggio had registered the name first and MV Agusta's 98cc motor cycle was instead marketed as the MV as were all subsequent MV Agusta-built motor cycles (and scooters).

Actually, Piaggio had chosen the Vespa name

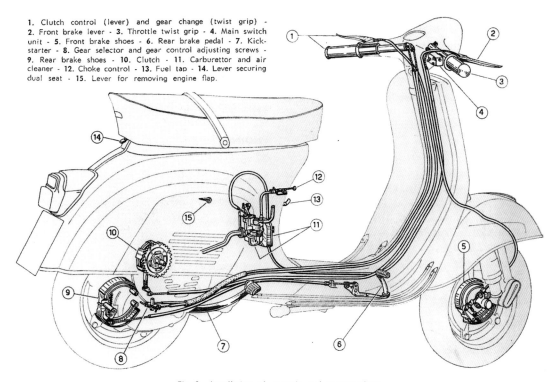

1. Clutch control (lever) and gear change (twist grip) -
2. Front brake lever - 3. Throttle twist grip - 4. Main switch
unit - 5. Front brake shoes - 6. Rear brake pedal - 7. Kick-
starter - 8. Gear selector and gear control adjusting screws -
9. Rear brake shoes - 10. Clutch - 11. Carburettor and air
cleaner - 12. Choke control - 13. Fuel tap - 14. Lever securing
dual seat - 15. Lever for removing engine flap.

Fig. 2 - Installation of controls and transmissions

*Until 1951, the Vespa gear change was controlled by a complicated rod linkage. Thereafter, as shown, it was replaced by cables, which were not only cheaper, but more efficient.*

not from the ancient Roman emperor Titus Flavius Sabinis Vespasianus, but rather because the buzzing of its two-stroke engine was akin to that of a wasp!

### First Public View and Early Production
The original Vespa made its first public bow at the 1946 Milan Spring Fair, and a total of 100 pre-production examples were constructed and tested prior to production itself that began later that year. By the end of December 1946, production (excluding prototypes and pre-production machines) totalled 2,484 examples.

### Technical Innovation
Strangely, it had been Pirelli's inability to supply Piaggio with transmission belts of sufficiently high quality to ensure continuing reliability (rubber being in short supply during the mid-1940s) that led to the decision to locate the gearbox and engine against the rear wheel, the resulting direct drive and the inline gearbox making it possible to create a compact engine/transmission/rear wheel assembly that was thereafter to remain one of the Vespa's outstanding features.

As D'Ascanio, ably assisted by another engineer, Mario D'Este, had no previous motor cycle experience, he chose aviation rather than conventional two-wheel practices. As D'Ascanio commented:

> For several fundamental solutions on the Vespa, I took inspiration from various aeronautic approaches with which I was familiar, such as for instance the monotube support for the rear wheel … As far as the frame was concerned, I found myself working well beyond the most modern automotive concepts, because the sheet-metal bodywork also served as [the] frame-work, and because of its special manufacturing it provided greater strength and resistance than the old tube-based system. Here too my experience in the field of aeronautics helped me, in that field lightness of structure must not interfere with its sturdiness.

*The Press Launch*
Although, as already outlined, the public's first view of the Vespa came at the Milan Fair, the press and government officials got to see it earlier, in February 1946 – the venue, the prestigious Rome Golf Club. Strangely enough, the guest of honour chosen to send the newcomer on its way was not an Italian, but the American General Stone, representing the Allied military occupation governmental body. The event was also filmed by the American film news service, Movie Tone.

*Marketing and Distribution*
Piaggio required an entirely fresh way of marketing its new product. As *Vespa From Italy with Love* (Giorgio Nada Editore, 2000)

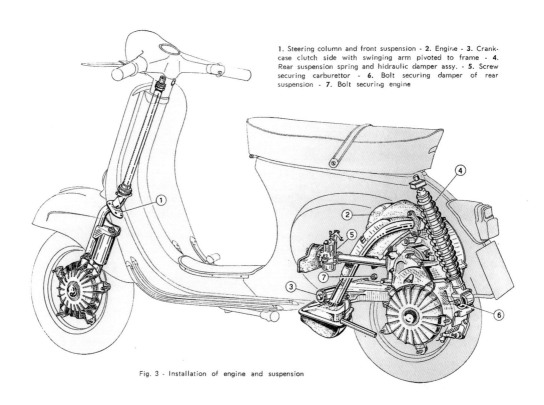

1. Steering column and front suspension - 2. Engine - 3. Crankcase clutch side with swinging arm pivoted to frame - 4. Rear suspension spring and hidraulic damper assy. - 5. Screw securing carburettor - 6. Bolt securing damper of rear suspension - 7. Bolt securing engine

Fig. 3 - Installation of engine and suspension

*Installation of engine, exhaust and suspension.*

explained, 'The Vespa ... was a product designed for a far broader and more fragmented market. It was therefore necessary to invent an entirely new distribution network.'

Interestingly, Enrico Piaggio had approached the old-established motor cycle firm Moto Guzzi – and it appears that Piaggio would have probably been willing to market the new scooter under the Guzzi brand name. However, after several meetings between the two firms, Guzzi withdrew – reasoning that the Vespa was a product without a future. Of course, with the benefit of hindsight, this can

be judged to have probably been the biggest mistake in the history of powered two-wheeled transport!

### A New Sales Approach

And so Piaggio were forced into doing the job of marketing and distribution themselves. They began by sending executives into the retail sector, notably Lancia car showrooms (Lancia being chosen because of its up-market image at that time).

As one commentator said, 'Each of the car salesmen were asked to commit to a certain minimum number of Vespas. The idea worked.' And this is how the innovative scooter was initially sold to the public.

### Foreign Interest

Even the British motor cycle press noticed the Vespa. *Motor Cycle* dated 31 October 1946 reported that:

> An Italian two-wheeled runabout, the 98cc Vespa, made by Piaggio S.A. of Genoa, had many novel and interesting features. Its small wheels, low pressure tyres and general enclosure make it specially attractive for town and short-distance work. Moreover, the Vespa may be equipped with a carrier, a saddle-type, pillion seat ... and spare wheel, or a trailer.

By the autumn of 1946, the 98cc (50x50mm) Piaggio-made engine with three speeds (this having replaced the original Sachs unit employed in the *Paperino*), flywheel magneto ignition and fan-cooling (the latter generated by blades on the outside of the flywheel rotor) had sparked considerable interest both at home and abroad.

### Worried Rivals

The Vespa also generated fear from the established Italian motor cycle industry, which immediately attempted to deride the newcomer. Piaggio themselves dismissed these

*The 1966 90SS (Super Sprint), available in Monza red or peacock blue. It could reach 56mph (90km/h).*

*The weird and wonderful Vespa military model. The French dropped these by parachute and then fitted 75mm cannons, whilst the Italian army fitted bazookas!*

attacks, claiming (correctly) that the Vespa was not a small cousin of the motor cycle, but rather an entirely new form of transportation intended for slower speeds and shorter distances. And as experience was to prove, Piaggio had come up with a winning formula. As fellow author Michael Dregni pointed out, 'The most unique feature of the scooter was the step-through frame, flat footboards, and full bodywork to protect the rider from the elements.'

## Evolution

The first Vespa models featured the headlamp mounted on the front mudguard that turned with the wheel and handlebars that followed motor cycle practice by being left bare. Later, the headlamp was moved, first to the top of the front apron just below the handlebars, and later still mounted directly to the handlebars with all cabling enclosed. It should also be explained

that from 1946 until the end of 1951, the Vespa gear change was controlled by a complicated rod linkage. From 1952 onwards this was replaced by cables, which was not only much simpler and cheaper, but more efficient too. These early machines were known as the 'rod-type'.

Other important events in the evolution of the Vespa series included a larger 124 85cc (56.5x49.8mm) engine in 1948, and a brand-new 150cc (57x57mm) four-speed model in 1954. But the high point of the classic Vespa scooter was without doubt the 150 *Gran Sport* (GS) that made its début in a blaze of glory in November 1954, before being superseded from the 1962 model year by the larger-engined 160 GS.

## Mass Production

Production figures tell the story of just how successful the Vespa series really was:

# vespa

## 100 CC.

PIAGGIO

## technical specifications

Speed: 70 Km/h (CUNA Standards) - Fuel consumption with 2% oil mixture: 1.8 lts. per 100 Km. - Max. climbing gradient: 30% - Carrying capacity: 2 persons - Engine: single cylinder, two-stroke with rotating type induction; bore: 49 mm. - stroke: 51 mm. - Displacement: 96,12 cu. cm. - Gearbox: 3 speed with constant mesh gears - Max. length: 1665 mm. - Max. width: 670 mm. - Wheel base: 1180 mm. - Max. height: 1015 mm. - Curb weight: 73 Kg.

Höchstgeschwindigkeit: 70 Km/h (CUNA-Normen) - Verbrauch: (Mischung mit 2% Öl) 1,8 Liter/100 Km - Maximale Steigfähigkeit: 30% - Tragfähigkeit: 2 Personen - Motor: Einzylinder Zweitaktmotor mit Drehschiebersteuerung - Bohrung: 49 mm. - Hub: 51 mm. - Hubraum: 96,12 ccm. - 3 Gangschaltung - Länge: 1665 mm., Breite 670 mm., Radstand: 1180 mm. - Höhe: 1015 mm. - Leergewicht: 73 Kg.

Vitesse: 70 Km/h (normes CUNA) - Consommation (mélange 2% d'huile): 1,8 litres aux 100 Km. - Pente franchissable: 30% - Portée: 2 personnes - Moteur: monocylindrique, 2 temps, à distribution rotative - alésage: 49 mm. - course: 51 mm. - Cylindrée: 96,12 cc. - Boîte de vitesse: à 3 vitesses - Longueur maximum: 1665 mm. - Largeur maximum: 670 mm. - Empattement: 1180 mm. - Hauteur maximum: 1015 mm. - Poids à vide: 73 Kg.

Velocidad: 70 Km/hs (normas CUNA) - Consumo (mezcla con 2% de aceite): 1,8 litros cada 100 Km. - Pendiente máxima superable: 30% - Cabida para 2 personas - Motor monocilindrico de 2 tiempos, con distribución rotativa - Diámetro del cilindro: 49 mm. - Carrera: 51 mm. - Cilindrada: 96,12 cc. - Cambio: de 4 velocidades - Longitud máxima: 1665 mm. - Anchura máxima: 670 mm. - Distancia entre ejes: 1180 mm. - Altura máxima: 1015 mm. - Peso en vacío: 73 Kg.

(Full rights of any modification, reserved)

*The 90 was eventually replaced by the 100, which was capable of only 47mph (76km/h), but it continued the successful Vespa formula of engineering and styling in equal measure.*

| Year | Model | Production |
|---|---|---|
| 1945 | *Paperino* prototype | 1 |
| 1946 | 98cc Vespa pre-production prototypes | 100 |
| 1946 | 98cc Vespa production models | 2,484 |
| 1947 | 98cc | 10,535 |
| 1948 | 125cc | 19,822 |
| 1949 | 125cc | 35,578 |
| 1950 | 125cc | 61,881 |
| 1951 | 125cc | 75,141 (affected by strikes) |
| 1952 | 125cc | 89,893 |
| 1953 | 125cc | 100,708 |
| 1954 | 125 & 150cc | 107,470 |
| 1955 | 125 & 150cc | 103,834 |
| 1956 | 125 & 150cc | 122,493 |

The above refers to Italian production only.

The *Gran Sport* GS150 made its bow at the Milan Show in late 1954. It was soon given the nickname of *Vespone* (big wasp). And because of its sporting nature, it immediately became one of Vespa's most popular models.

*First introduced for the 1955 season, the Vespa GS150 soon won a deserved reputation for exciting performance and its turbine-smooth 145cc engine.*

Besides its larger capacity engine and four-speed transmission, it also featured a dual seat and was the first Vespa to have the larger 10in wheels. But most important of all for speed-minded Italians, it could reach 100km/h under favourable conditions.

The GS had been built due to the demand for more powerful scooters, particularly for the two-up work. The first production series of the GS was designated the Vespa Sports 1 (VS1), and from then on the GS150 was given yearly updates until 1959, with the definitive VS5 version, production of which continued until 1962, when it was replaced by the new GS160.

The 145cc engine of the GS was not, as many thought, a bored-out version of the existing 124cc unit, instead both bore and stroke dimensions were increased, each being 57mm compared with the smaller engine's 'square', 54mm size. Carburation was taken care of by a Dell'Orto UB23 instrument. Compression ratio of the GS engine was 7:1, and Piaggio claimed a power output of 8bhp at 7,500rpm. The gearbox was given a closer ratio four-speed cluster, but the change was still operated by the familiar twist-grip-cum-clutch control on the nearside (left) handlebar.

*A new, larger GS, the 160 made its début at the Milan Show in late 1961. The big change was an additional 13cc, giving 158cc.*

The well-proved integral chassis-body construction was retained but there were several noticeable differences from earlier Vespas. Amongst these was the restyling of the engine fairing, which now provided a more complete enclosure and was louvered to assist cooling. There was also the aforementioned dual seat.

Deeper curvature of the weather shield greatly enhanced the appearance and, by reducing turbulence round the sides, not only provided superior aerodynamics but also improved weather protection. Another major change was placing the headlamp above the weather shield, so that it now turned with the handlebars – a feature to be used forthwith on future Vespa models.

As before, both wheels were of the bolt-on pattern carried on stub axles, so that wheel removal or replacement was an extremely quick and easy task. The rim size had been increased, to improve handling at higher speeds, tyres being of 3.50 section front and rear.

A notable change occurred for the 1959 model year, when the GS150 was given finned light-alloy brake drums retained by a large central nut on both front and rear hubs.

*Motor Cycling* tested an example of the latest GS150 in its 17 March 1960 issue and commented that:

> For the scooterist who longs for a sports car but cannot afford one, the GS is the perfect answer: for the scooterist who wants a fast and comfortable scooter without going into the large-capacity bracket, it is every bit as suitable and its price of well under £200 – £188 8s 3d, (including British taxes) makes it an extremely attractive proposition.

All models of the GS150 were produced in a metallic silver grey finish.

A new, larger GS, the 160, made its début at the Milan Show in late 1961. First supplies arrived in Great Britain during the spring of 1962. The big change was an additional 13cc, bore and stroke dimensions now being 58x60mm, giving 158cc.

Although the claimed power output was virtually unchanged at 8.2bhp, the engine torque figures were now much flatter, resulting in better low-speed pulling.

An unusual feature was that the main bearings were not petrol-lubricated. Instead the bearing on the generator side was prepacked with grease, and on the drive side the bearing was lubricated by splash from the transmission case.

Changes had been made to the front fork, a single telescopic unit replacing separate spring and hydraulic units. And following latest Italian scooter fashion, the width of the weather shield had been substantially reduced. A neat touch was the spare wheel storage beneath the nearside blister; previously the optional spare wheel had been carried at the rear of the windshield.

At the end of 1964 Piaggio announced that the GS160 had been taken out of production and was to be replaced by the 180cc Super Sport (SS). The newcomer was virtually identical to the machine it replaced apart from a few alterations

to the lines of the bodywork and a larger engine, with bore and stoke dimensions of 62x60mm respectively. Piaggio sources claimed 9.6bhp at 6,250rpm and a speed of 65mph (104.5km/h).

However, to this day, to many, the original GS150 was the one that embodied the Vespa concept in its truest form. Scooter historian Mike Webster explains why:

> Although produced in volume, this is one scooter that is avidly collected worldwide. Even so, fanatical motorcyclists, who would deride all scooters on principle, have been known to make an exception after trying the GS. They concede that this, at least, is a true classic with outstanding abilities.

| Specification | 1958 Vespa GS150 |
|---|---|
| Engine | Fan-cooled, two-stroke, single |
| Displacement | 145.45cc |
| Bore & stroke | 57x57mm |
| Gearbox | four speed, twist-grip change |
| Wheel size | 10in |
| Power | 8bhp |
| Maximum speed | 60mph (96.5km/h) |

The brochure says it all: 'The scooter for the man who wants Power Speed & Performance with Safety'.

## Vespa Goes Worldwide

In April 1956, the one-millionth Vespa was produced, combining the production of all its factories, including France, Great Britain, and West Germany, which were by this time building Vespas under licence. A celebration was staged at Piaggio's Italian Pontedera plant and Vespa Day was declared throughout Italy, with festivities held in no fewer than fifteen Italian cities, including a convoy of over 2,000 Vespas travelling *en masse* through Rome and halting all traffic. By then the Vespa had become more than simply a means of transport, but a movement with avid followers all over the world.

The Vespa was now not just a means of getting from A to B cheaply and reliably, but it had taken part in races and rallies too – even breaking world speed records. There were countless Vespa clubs throughout Europe and the dealer network was truly vast. Certainly in Italy servicing facilities were everywhere, making for a pleasurable ownership experience even if one wasn't interested in becoming a club member.

As far as 'foreign' Vespas were concerned, these came in two categories: Italian-built machines exported abroad (for example both Cushman and Sears imported the Italian scooters into the USA); or more commonly, at least in Europe, under licence agreements.

The latter included:

| | |
|---|---|
| West Germany | Hoffman (mid-1949–55) |
| | Messerschmitt (1955–mid-1960s) |
| Great Britain | Douglas★ (1951–64) |
| France | *Ateliers de Construction de Motocycles et d'Accessories* (ACMA) (1951–62) |
| Belgium | Motor Industry SA (1950s–60s) |
| Chile | Spencer & Cio (exact dates unknown) |
| Spain | Vespa SA (1962 onwards) |

★ Thereafter Douglas imported machines direct from Italy.

ALWAYS THE CENTRE OF ATTRACTION THROUGHOUT THE WORLD.

Douglas Vespa 125cc THE TWO WHEEL CAR

OWN A VESPA & ENJOY TRAVEL INDEPENDENCE

STAND No. 9 MAIN HALL

DOUGLAS (SALES AND SERVICE) LTD., KINGSWOOD, BRISTOL

*From 1951, the Bristol-based Douglas concern built Vespas under licence in Great Britain. All Douglas-Vespas had the headlamp mounted on the apron (or later, the handlebars); whereas the early Italian-built machines had it mounted on the front mudguard.*

Later, and outside the scope of this book, although the main production facilities were to remain at Pontedera, new plants sprang up in India, the People's Republic of China, Taiwan, Indonesia, Thailand, Iran, Pakistan, Tunisia, Egypt, the Czech Republic, the Congo and Venezuela.

at the right time. It was also a revolutionary design that has stood the test of time and required surprisingly little development over the years, so correct was D'Ascanio's creation in the first place.

The Vespa also caught the public's imagination. Whereas a particular sports motor cycle

*The German agent produced this colourful brochure with the youth market very much in mind.*

By 1993, Piaggio had built ten million Vespas world-wide – millions more than its closest rival, Innocenti, whose Lambrettas only totalled some four million. And of course the brand is a continuing success story and is today the largest manufacturer of powered two-wheelers outside Japan.

### Why The Success?

So why was Vespa so successful? The answer is actually multi-faceted. It was the right product

*Miss Lazio, seen with a Vespa and Sophia Loren publicity, circa mid-1950.*

*Piaggio always viewed the youth market as its number one target.*

model might be an icon to the enthusiastic few, the Vespa's appeal was truly universal.

Another reason for this success was what one Italian journalist referred to as the 'message', that advertising was the 'soul of the Vespa'. And like Honda years later with its 'You meet the nicest people on a Honda' slogan, so, in the immediate post-war years, Piaggio produced a series of highly creative and successful marketing stunts and visually exciting adverts and posters – there was even an annual Vespa calendar, the latter combining female glamour with the ever-present Vespa.

Piaggio also always promoted the Vespa as having a certain upper-class status – even though it was affordable by almost anyone.

They began, as previously mentioned, by selling the product through Lancia showrooms – so giving the impression that the customer was buying a distinctive, distinguished product.

But without doubt Piaggio's ace card was what today would be referred to as 'product placement'. Wherever possible, the company would pair the Vespa with a celebrity, especially a film star. No-one can forget the Vespas that Audrey Hepburn and Gregory Peck rode in the film *Roman Holiday*. During the boom sales period of the 1950s it seemed that wherever there were celebrities there was the accompanying Vespa scooter. Similarly, with the pop culture that followed, the Vespa was just as prevalent. And so the Vespa became a legend in its own lifetime.

this time to the industrial north and the Milanese suburb of Lambrate. Here, he founded a steel company that would be the basis of his future empire. However, the Lambrate plant was almost totally destroyed during the Second World War, so Innocenti faced the daunting task of not only rebuilding his facilities, but also finding a profitable niche of the metal finishing market in which to sell his wares.

## The Lambretta is Born

During the Second World War, Innocenti had manufactured artillery shells and pontoon bridges, but with the end of the war in sight, Innocenti and his general director, Giuseppe Lauro, looked for an alternative peacetime product. Like Piaggio – but without either organization knowing what the other was considering – Innocenti began experimenting with the idea of producing a scooter. The thought behind producing such a machine was simply that most people could afford to own and operate such a device.

*Piaggio were always keen to associate the Vespa with celebrities.*

*The original 1947 Lambretta model A was 125 c.c. and had no rear suspension*

*The original 1947 Lambretta Model A featured a naked engine and transmission, plus an un-sprung frame.*

## Lambretta

Throughout the period covered by this book, the Vespa's main rival was the Lambretta.

Piaggio's opposite number and the inspiration behind the Lambretta was Ferdinando Innocenti. The youthful Innocenti had established his own workshop at the tender age of eighteen. In 1922, then aged thirty-one, he moved to Rome where he developed ways of improving the manufacture of steel tubing. Nine years later, in 1931, he moved once again,

# Iambretta 150cc D/56

**£108 : 4 : 7** plus **£25 : 19 : 6 P.Tax** P/SEAT EXTRA

*In 1954, Innocenti introduced its largest engine to date, displacing 148cc (57x58mm). A 1956 150D is shown.*

During 1945 and 1946, Innocenti and Lauro instructed one of their engineers, Pierluigi Torre, to create a scooter. They chose the name Lambretta after the plant's site, Lambrate – the area being thus named due to the bubbling brown Lambrate river that runs through the suburb, and now, due to the concentration of industrial sites, one of the most polluted in Italy.

## Model A

As related earlier, the first Vespa, the 98cc, went on sale during the spring of 1946. Lambretta's first scooter, the Model A, made its début in October 1947. And such was its success that within a year the 10,000th machine had rolled off the Lambrate production line.

Compared with the Vespa, the new Lambretta was not revolutionary in concept or radical in design. Instead it was well-built and reliable in service, and, most important of all, provided inexpensive transportation with ease of operation.

What the Model A lacked in outright style and technical innovation, it made up for with a larger engine – this displacing 125cc (52x58mm). And unlike the Vespa, the cooling for the power unit was simply by air (fan operation did not come until the LC model arrived in April 1950). And thus the A's engine was left uncovered. Other notable features included 7in wheels with 3.50 section tyres, a foot-operated three-speed gearbox, and a mixture of a tubular frame together with a pressed-steel box section to which the front of the engine was bolted. The entire rear of the machine was supported on the engine castings. The seat, fuel tank and rear storage box were mounted on two tubular rails, bolted to a box section with the seat clamped above. Unlike the comprehensive protection from the elements and mechanical parts of the Vespa, the Model A only offered tiny leg shields, these being bolted to the centre spine.

The most notable feature of the design was the long aluminium case housing the shaft drive and bevel gear set that drove the rear wheel. Suspension was simple in the extreme, being provided by springs within the saddle seat!

Besides the larger engine size, the Model A's other advantage over the original Vespa was its second seat and additional pulling power.

But overall the Model A was not really what buyers wanted – even though it found customers relatively easily in what was a seller's market. And so, in December 1948, Innocenti replaced it with the Model B.

**Models B, C and LC**
The A evolved into the B with a series of changes – larger 8in wheels, a nearside (left) twist-grip gear change employing a push-pull cable system, rather than the A's foot lever and, in an effort to compete more favourably with the Vespa, rear suspension. This suspension

*The LD150 was the fully enclosed version of the D.*

33

Innocenti launched the first of its TV *Turismo Veloce* (touring speed) models, the Series 1 TV175, at the Milan Spring Fair in April 1957, with production beginning the following September.

The engine-gear unit represented the first radical design departure made by Lambretta since the first of its scooters was introduced in the early post-war years. Most obvious was that the cylinder (bore and stroke being square at 60mm) was horizontal whilst the primary transmission was partly by chain.

Cooling from a fan as the flywheel generator of the 170cc power plant, directed air on the light-alloy cylinder head and iron barrel. The clutch was mounted on the offside (right) mainshaft and outboard of it was the engine sprocket with an outrigger bearing. A duplex chain transferred the drive to a sprocket incorporating the kick-starter mechanism just ahead of the twist-grip-controlled, four-speed gearbox, the output shaft of which formed the rear wheel stub axle. Drive reduction between the sprocket shaft and the gearbox was by two spur gears. The engine, light-alloy transmission case and wheel formed a pivoted unit controlled

*Innocenti launched the first of its TV models in 1957, the Series 1 having a 170cc engine.*

by a large-diameter coil spring of different rating surrounding a hydraulic damper.

But in construction the TV175 did not break away from previous Lambretta practice of a tubular frame with virtually unstressed bodywork. The main member was a single, large-diameter tube running from the steering head downwards in a shallow tunnel in the weather shield and along the floor section of the scooter's bodywork, then upward and to the rear above the engine. Welded to the main member was the pivot for the engine-gear unit and the anchorage of the suspension leg.

The front fork was tubular with trailing links; coil springs operated in the fork legs and slim hydraulic dampers were external. Wheels and brakes were both of larger diameters than the existing LD125/150 models: on the TV175 the wheel diameter was 10in, with 3.50 section tyres. The brake drums featured radial fins to improve both rigidity and cooling.

An interesting detail was that air for the Dell'Orto carburettor was drawn through a chromium-plated grille in the rear of the body into the main frame member and then, via trunking and a flexible connection, to the carburettor via an air cleaner and 'calming' device.

The British launch of the TV175 took place in early February 1958. In a speech, Peter Agg, a director of Lambretta Concessionaires, disclosed that there were then over 200 special Lambretta service stations open in Great Britain, plus hundreds of dealers in the British network.

Tested by *Motor Cycle* in its 3 April 1958 issue, the headline read, 'An Elegant Scooter of Great Merit: High Standard of Comfort, Handling, Braking and Hill-Climbing'. The test ended with 'Without question the TV175 is one of the world's outstanding scooters. It is deliberately designed to appeal to a wide range of tasks and its success over a long period is assured.'

However, as events were to prove, TV175 Series 1 was not anywhere good enough and, according to Michael Dregni, it proved a 'dismal failure'. This was because it was under developed, being rushed into production before it should have been, due to the major success that had been enjoyed by Vespa's sporting GS150 model. And because of this the TV Series 1 was withdrawn after only sixteen months of production, due to an abysmal service record of unreliability.

But to give Innocenti their due, they undertook a massive development programme that

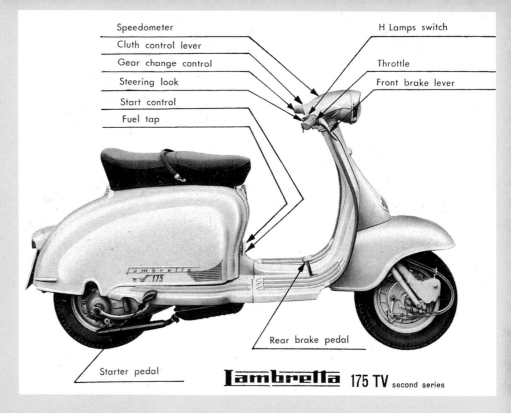

The much improved TV175 Series 2 arrived by the end of 1958, with its engine based on the Li150, rather than the problem-stricken Series 1 170cc unit.

Speedometer
Cluth control lever
Gear change control
Steering look
Start control
Fuel tap
H Lamps switch
Throttle
Front brake lever
Rear brake pedal
Starter pedal

**Lambretta** 175 TV second series

saw the arrival of the TV175 Series 2 on March 2 1959. However, this scooter was not based on the old model, but instead on the successful Li series. The only components transferred from the original were the name and the body style, but even the latter was updated. The newcomer could be easily identified by having its headlamp at handlebar height, rather than being incorporated into the apron; this also had the advantage that the light now turned with the handlebars.

*Motor Cycling & Scooter Weekly* published a test of the TV Series 2 in its 27 August 1959 issue. The engine now displaced 175cc. And to prove that this was no simple bore job, both the bore and stroke dimensions had been altered, to 62x58mm. Lambretta claimed 8.6bhp at 6,000rpm. And except for a change from 0.9in (23mm) down to 0.8in (20mm) in carburettor size (to provide a smoother spread of power) midway through production, the TV2 remained unchanged until replaced by the TV3 Slimline for the 1962 season.

The TV175 Series 3 not only adopted the new slimline style but gained slightly more power (8.7bhp), hydraulic front dampers for a smoother ride and, most significantly of all, a mechanically operated disc front brake.

Although this was not the first use of a disc set upon a powered two-wheeler (Maserati were first with their 250cc motor cycle in 1957), Lambretta were the first to use one on a mass-produced vehicle. The Series 3 ran until 1965.

The final TV model was the TV200 (also known as the GT200) that ran from 1963 through to 1965. Its 198cc capacity was achieved by increasing the bore size to 66mm, the stroke remaining unchanged at 58mm. And came mainly due to the efforts of the British importers. Power was up to 12bhp at 6,200rpm, giving a maximum speed of around 70mph (113km/h).

If one includes the TV200, total TV production was 106,565 units.

| Specification, | 1963 Lambretta TV175 Series 3 |
|---|---|
| Engine | Fan-cooled, two-stroke, single |
| Displacement | 175cc |
| Bore & stroke | 62x58mm |
| Gearbox | Four-speed, twist-grip change |
| Wheel size | 10in |
| Power | 8.7bhp |
| Maximum speed | 62mph (100km/h) |

The Lambretta Li series can in retrospect be seen as the last major sales success for Innocenti in the scooter market. From the first Li150 produced in April 1958 until the last of the series, the Li125 Series 3 Slimline, rolled off the Lambretta production line in May 1967, a total of 709,730 Li series scooters had been manufactured.

The original Li150, and the smaller Li125, which began production the following June, followed the same general styling as the TV175 Series 1.

The low-slung, horizontal, single-cylinder two-stroke engine followed the TV175 practice of driving through an oil-bath primary chain, with a four-speed, twist-grip-controlled gearbox located alongside the rear wheel. The earlier Lambretta shaft transmission and an engine-speed clutch, with their associated bevel gears, were thus dispensed with. The highly geared kick-starter, like that of a conventional motorcycle, acted through the gearbox, though this required a rearward location of the shaft.

A new design of gearbox, employing sliding cursors instead of dogs, ensured easy meshing without clashing, and without recourse to the clutch was a multi-plate assembly running in the primary case oil-bath.

Principal differences between the cycle parts of the Li and the LD models were in improved distribution of weight with larger tyres (10in instead of 8in) and more braking area on both wheels – almost double on the front wheel. As with the TV175, the brake drums were radially finned both for rapid heat dissipation and for stiffening; the drums were of light alloy, with iron liners for the braking surfaces.

Like the earlier Lambrettas, front suspension was by trailing links that had a multi-rate, helical spring enclosed within the fork stanchions, there being no damping. The rear suspension, which was of the swinging arm variety, with the transmission case doubling up as the arm (the engine also pivoted), was controlled by a single multi-rate unit.

The Li150 displaced 148cc (57x58mm) whilst the smaller Li125 measured 123cc (52x58mm); power outputs were 6.5bhp and 5.2bhp respectively.

Whereas the original TV175 was a failure, just the reverse was true of the Li 125/150 *Motor Cycling* dated 6 November 1958 commenting:

In the first mile of an extensive road test, the Li 150 gave an immediate impression of peppiness, power and rapid response from the new engine … The motor, although of the same bore, stroke and general characteristics as the LD unit, derives increased output from better crank case compression, 'hotter' porting and a higher working rpm – 5,300 for the peak power, whereas the LD's figure was 4,600rpm.

The Li series was updated in 1959 with the headlight relocated from the apron to the

*The Lambretta Li150 Series 1 was first produced in April 1958 and, together with the smaller capacity Li125, went on to become a major sales success story for Innocenti.*

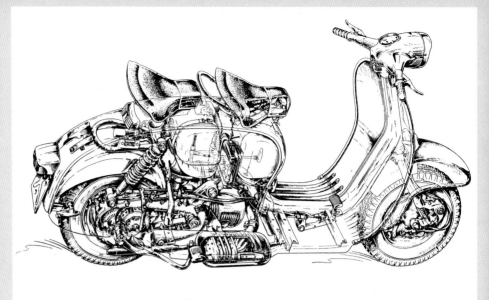

*Artist's drawing of the Li Series 2.*

**Lambretta li** second series

handlebars (as on the TV175 Series 2). The Li125 Series 2 engine breathed through a 0.7in (18mm) Dell'Orto carburettor, whereas the 150 did the same via a 0.8in (20mm) instrument. In addition there had been modifications to the air intake and cylinder porting.

Then, for the 1962 model year, the Li125/150 Series 3 arrived. A major styling change was introduced called 'slimstyle', this giving sleek and angular lines rather than the rounder lines of the Series 1 and 2 machines. There were also power increases: the 125 giving 5.5bhp, the 150 6.6bhp.

Besides the standard 1, 2 and 3 Series Li machines there were some rather special versions. One of the most interesting was the Li150 Rally Master that the British importers offered in 1962. It was, as the name suggests, fully equipped for rallying – including a tachometer, a plastic waterproof case for a stop-watch, a spare wheel behind the dashboard, competition plate holders, a small Perspex screen, a new front mudguard and ball-end control levers.

There was also the Li150 Pacemaker (1963–66) with more power (7.6bhp at 5,600rpm) and revised gear ratios.

If one includes all the special editions, production of the various Li series topped a million units. And this figure only includes Italian production at its Lambrate plant.

*The Li series was updated in 1959 with the headlamp relocated from the apron to the handlebars (as on the TV175 Series 2). The machine shown here dates from 1962.*

| Specification | 1959 Lambretta Li150 Series 1 |
|---|---|
| Engine | Fan-cooled, two-stroke, single |
| Displacement | 148cc |
| Bore & Stroke | 57x58mm |
| Gearbox | Four-speed, twist-grip change |
| Wheel size | 10in |
| Power | 6.5bhp |
| Maximum speed | 52mph (84km/h) |

The Li150 (and Li125) replaced the LD series. This is an advertisement for the Lambretta stand at the London Earls Court Show in November 1958.

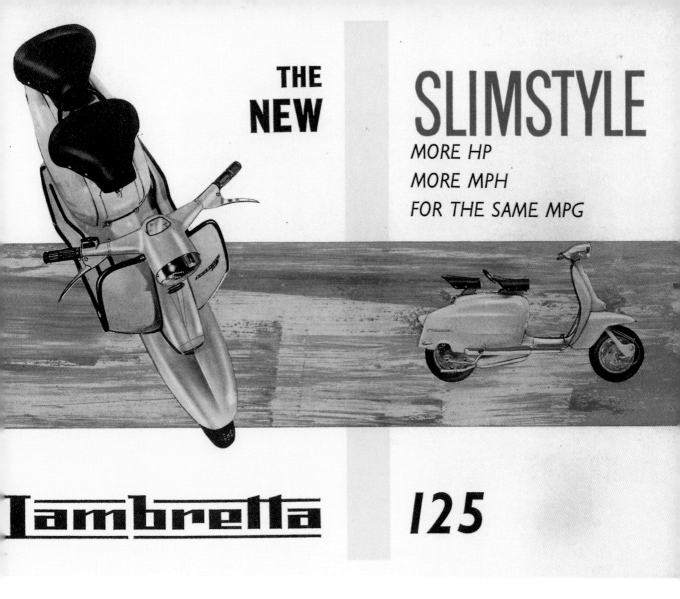

THE NEW **SLIMSTYLE**

MORE HP
MORE MPH
FOR THE SAME MPG

**Lambretta** *125*

*The Li (and TV) series were subsequently built in Series 2 and Series 3 (also known as the Slimstyle) versions. The Li Series 1 ran from 1958–59; Series 2, 1959–61; Series 3, Li125 1961–67, and Li150 1962–67.*

operated via a swinging knuckle on the rear of the shaft drive housing casing controlled by a coil-spring damper unit mounted horizontally under the engine. These changes made the Model B into a bestseller, Innocenti building 100 machines a day.

But if the B was an improvement on the A, the C that followed was even better, being essentially a tried and tested 4.3bhp shaft-drive engine in a redesigned chassis. Produced from

February 1950 to November 1951, the earlier A/B twin-tube construction type was replaced by a single large-diameter tube wrapped around the engine and fuel tank to support the two seats.

From April 1950 it was possible to purchase the LC *Lusso* (luxury) model. This not only featured – for the first time on a Lambretta – rear enclosure, but also fan cooling.

*At the 1961 Milan Show, Innocenti displayed a prototype 50cc scooter. This was followed by a 100cc production version named the Cento. Shortly afterwards this gave way to the J (Junior) series. One of the three-speed J125 models is shown here. This was subsequently upgraded and sold from 1966–69 with four gears.*

## The D Series

In December 1951 the D/LD 125 arrived. These featured a redesigned frame, front fork tubes that enclosed the front suspension springs, larger section tyres (4.00 instead of 3.50), and a new rear suspension set-up that saw the engine hung by pivoting links and suspended at the rear by a single damper. The engine's output had also been increased from 4.30bhp at 4,500rpm to 4.8bhp at 4,600rpm, and a 0.7in (18mm) instead of a 0.6in (15mm) Dell'Orto carburettor was specified. An electric start version of the LD125 was also offered from February 1954, but this was not a success as it added both cost and weight, as was also the case with the later LD150 electric start variant.

Compared with the LC125, the LD introduced a two-piece sheet-steel pressing to direct cooling air over the cylinder barrel and heat from the fan. Externally, it was possible to tell the LC and LD apart thanks to oval side panel grilles, which replaced the twin 'portholes' employed on the LC. It should be pointed out that the similar 125E (April 1953–February 1954) and 125F (March 1954–April 1955) models were also offered.

## A Larger Engine

From autumn 1954, Innocenti introduced its largest displacement scooter to date, the 148cc (57x58mm). This put out a claimed 6bhp at 4,750rpm, whilst the flywheel magneto was up-rated from 25 watts on the 125 Series to 36 watts. And although the 150 added 5mph (8km/h) to the maximum speed, fuel consumption was cut by some 25 per cent.

Innocenti's next move saw the introduction of the brand-new 175TV (from April 1957), the Li150 (from April 1958) and the Li125 (from June 1958) models.

The TV/Li series were subsequently built in Series 2 and Series 3 versions and from April 1963, a 200TV (also referred to as the GT200) arrived. This put out 12bhp at 6,200rpm and could reach 70mph (113km/h). To achieve the additional displacement for the 200, the cylinder bore size was increased from 62 to 66mm on the TV175 Series 2/3 machines.

*Next came the Lui series, built as the 50cc Luna, the 75cc Vega and the 75cc Cometa. The trio were the work of Italian styling house Bertone and were intended to provide Lambretta with a new, more modern appearance.*

### Foreign Lambrettas

Like Piaggio, Innocenti licensed several foreign companies to produce locally built Lambrettas. The most notable are as follows:

| | |
|---|---|
| West Germany | NSU (1950–55) |
| France | *Société Industrielle de Troyes* (SIT) (from 1952) |
| Argentina | Siambretta (1950s–60s) |
| Spain | ★(from 1952; with production beginning in 1954) |
| India | Scooters India (from 1972) |

★Originally the machines were marketed as Lambrettas, but were later renamed Servettas.

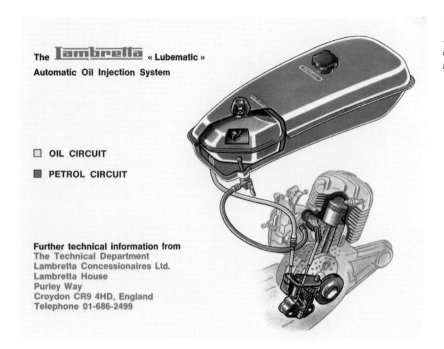

The 75cc Cometa featured the
Lubematic automatic (pump)
oil injection system — a first for
the Italian scooter industry.

The **Lambretta** « Lubematic »
**Automatic Oil Injection System**

☐ OIL CIRCUIT

■ PETROL CIRCUIT

**Further technical information from
The Technical Department
Lambretta Concessionaires Ltd.
Lambretta House
Purley Way
Croydon CR9 4HD, England
Telephone 01-686-2499**

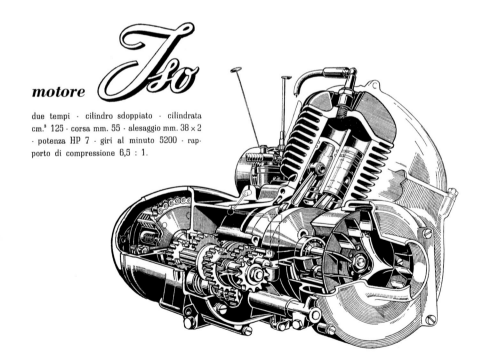

**motore** *Iso*

due tempi · cilindro sdoppiato · cilindrata
cm.³ 125 · corsa mm. 55 · alesaggio mm. 38 × 2
· potenza HP 7 · giri al minuto 5200 · rap-
porto di compressione 6,5 : 1.

A cutaway drawing of the
ISO split-single two-stroke
engine with fan-cooling, as
used on the early scooters from
that marque.

*The January 1969 issue of Motorcycle Mechanics tested the Vega (they called it a Luna!) and, except for a weak front brake, praised the machine.*

JANUARY 1969                    2/6d

# MOTORCYCLE
### SCOOTER & THREE-WHEELER
# MECHANICS
## LARGEST SALE

# OVER-THE-COUNTER
# SPEED!

BONNEVILLE AND
LAMBRETTA '69 TESTS
CAPRI STRIP            POWER TOOL TIPS
BETTER BOUNCE CONTROL     RIDE SAFE!

# FREE CONTINENTAL TRIP!  SPECIAL M.M. CONTEST INSIDE

Innocenti were also involved in industrial ventures in Argentina, Brazil, Mexico and the USA.

## Never Just Scooters

Innocenti never restricted itself to simply scooters. Over the years it continued its original steel tube business as well as manu-facturing milling machines and presses. Another important source of revenue was the production of components for the majority of Italian car makers, as well as the European arm of the Ford Motor Company and the German Volkswagen group. Yet another was car manu-facture itself, notably of the Italian version of the legendary British Mini.

# The ISO Diva (Milano)

In their book the *Motor Scooter Buyer's Guide,* brothers Michael and Eric Dregni stated that, 'In 1957, ISO created its masterpiece, the Diva scooter … The styling was graceful with bodacious, flowing curves from the front tender to the side covers. The look was half-Vespa, half-Lambretta TV1; the effect was inspiring.'

The Diva made its début at the 35th Milan Show in late 1957. Unlike earlier ISO twin-piston engines, the new unit was a fan-cooled 146cc (57x57mm) two-stroke of single piston layout with a chain-driven, four-speed gearbox in the unit. Final drive was by a duplex chain in a light-alloy case supporting the stub axle and rear wheel and forming the rear suspension arm.

As on the Lambretta, the main frame comprised a single tube from the steering head. From its middle location under the floor, the tube curved upward at the nearside (left) of the engine and additional tubes and lugs supported the engine pivot and the body. The front wheel was supported by a trailing arm controlled, like the rear suspension, by a single spring-and-

hydraulic unit. Tyre size was 3.50x10.

First export supplies reached Great Britain in early 1958. The British model differed slightly from the Italian version in being fitted with a dual seat, having a shrouded handlebar and a direct 6-volt (flywheel magneto) lighting and parking battery, rather than a charging set. The importers were Stewart & Payne of London. The price, including British taxes, was £175 14s 6d.

*Motor Cycle* tested an example of the Diva in its 1 May 1958 issue, beginning:

> Very much in the Italian tradition, the ISO has clean lines, small dimensions and relatively low weight. In construction it is both orthodox and sturdy and it possesses in good measure qualities which make the machine most suitable for its intended purpose. The seat height and general riding position are comfortable and all controls are well sited with the possible exception of the front-brake lever, which is mounted a trifle low … The combination of lightness, good pulling power and a four-speed gearbox made the ISO a lively proposition in traffic … the good performance and handling were matched by brakes of ample power.

Rivals *Motor Cycle News* in its 23 April 1958 issue commented:

> One of the most endearing features of the 146cc four-speed ISO, and a factor which would be more appreciated by the owner who makes this delightful little scooter his or her 'first', is its complete absence of transmission snatch, not only in the case of gearchanging, which is simplicity itself, but when power is reapplied on the overrun.

Milano Model

Complete with saver borders and rear side panel grilles.

*Retail Price*
**£166 - 19 - 6**
Including Purchase Tax

**ISO**

**The 150 cc. 4 speed scooter**

*Along with the Vespa and Lambretta, the 146cc (57x57mm) Diva was one of the mainstream Italian scooters of its era.*

A feature of the Diva was easy accessibility. By removing six nuts, the entire rear of the machine, including engine, transmission, frame and suspension could be exposed to facilitate maintenance.

Running on a compression ratio of 6.5:1, power output was 6bhp at 5,000rpm. Lubrication was by petroil mixture: 16:1 during the first 500 miles (805km); 20:1 thereafter. The maximum speed was 52mph (84km/h).

A de Luxe version made its début in spring 1959. The basic design remained as before, but the carburettor and silencer had been

## Technical Features

Max. ground clearance mm. 1050 (handlebar) (41")
Min. ground clearance mm. 140 (5 ½")
Max. length mm. 1760 (69")
Wheel base mm. 1280 (50 ½")
Max. width mm. 740 (handlebar) (29")
Seat clearance from ground mm. 800 (31½")
**Induction filter:** air intake outside the body; box for silencing, purifying and decanting the air
**Engine:** Single cylinder, two stroke
**Bore:** mm. 57 (2⁵/₁₆")
**Piston stroke:** mm. 57 (2⁵/₁₆")
**Cylinder volume:** 146 cc.
**Power:** 6 B. H. P.
**Maximum R.P.M.:** 5000
**Compression ratio:** 6,5 : 1
**Cooling:** by fan
**Lubrication:** by fuel-oil mixture
**Ignition:** by flywheel magneto, external coil
**Clutch:** multiple steel discs in oil bath
**Gearshift:** four speed - hand controlled by handlebar grip

**Kick starter:** Pedal controlled
**Drive:**
PRIMARY: by a chain in oil bath
SECONDARY: by a duplex chain in oil bath
**Frame:** high strength steel tubes
**Suspension:** front: swinging arm with hydraulic shock absorber
Rear: by engine-drive assembly swinging plus hydraulic shock absorber
**Brakes:** expansion type - drums Ø 5 ¾" (140 mm)
**Tyres:** 3.50 x 10
**Speedometer:** built into the headlight
**Tank capacity:** 1 ½ gallon of mixture including the reserve tank
**Engine inspection:** by two wide side inspection doors, easily removable
**Speed:** approx. 52 miles per hour (80 Km/h)
**Consumption:** 1 gallon per 105 miles (CUNA rules)
**Weight:** 215 lbs.

The above specifications are subject to alteration and the manufacturers do not hold themselves responsible for any variations.

*The Diva with a dual seat, as imported into Great Britain around 1960.*

redesigned and the bodywork had been cleaned up with the addition of side grilles, rubber saver borders round the weather shield and pillion footboard rubbers.

The price in Great Britain had, however, been reduced to £166 19s 6d.

| Specification | 1958 ISO Diva (Milano) |
|---|---|
| Engine | Fan-cooled, two-stroke, single |
| Displacement | 146cc |
| Bore & stroke | 57x57mm |
| Gearbox | Four-speed, twist-grip change |
| Wheel size | 10in |
| Power | 6bhp |
| Maximum speed | 55mph (88km/h) |

## The Power of The Brand Name

Like Piaggio with their Vespa brand name, Innocenti right from the start fostered the Lambretta name. This was achieved by several means: advertising in the press, radio and later on television; racing and record breaking; club activities and films to name but a few. Even now, at the beginning of the 21st century, the Lambretta logo is a valuable commodity – for example, being used to market a range of clothing.

## Italian Lambretta Production Ends

After Ferdinando Innocenti died in June 1966, scooter sales continued a slide that had begun in 1962, and even though Lambretta tried hard to combat this trend by advertising and the release of new models, including the Cento 100, GT 200, SX 200 and 122cc Starstream, the rot continued.

Lambretta production at Lambrate ceased in 1971 (although production continued abroad, notably in Spain and India, the latter purchasing the Italian tooling in 1972). And then, in 1975, the Innocenti group was taken over by the Argentinian-Italian industrialist Alejandro de Tomaso, who added the Lambrate factory to his extensive portfolio, which by that time included Benelli and Moto Guzzi motor cycles plus Maserati and De Tomaso cars.

## Isothermos

Following the successes achieved first by Piaggio with their Vespa, and then the Innocenti Lambretta, the next Italian company to enter the scooter field was Isothermos (ISO). Founded by Renzo Rivolta at Bresso in 1939, the fledgling organization had hardly begun trading when production plans were halted by the outbreak of the Second World War.

At first, ISO's production centred around refrigerators. But like Enrico Piaggio and Ferdinando Innocenti, Renzo Rivolta realized the need in Italy in the aftermath of the War for affordable personal transportation.

## Early Models

The first ISO scooter, the *Furetto* of 1948–49 was powered by a 65cc single-cylinder two-stroke engine. However, even Renzo Rivolta hated it, and so it was quickly axed in favour of two new designs. Although they were listed as the Isoscooter and Isomoto (motor cycle), both machines come into the scope of this book. This was because the *Moto* was in reality half-scooter, half-motor cycle with small, 3.00x12 tyres and comprehensive bodywork. Meanwhile the Isoscooter was a genuine scooter, but with a somewhat ungainly style.

Both models shared an identical 124.7cc two-stroke split-single-cylinder engine clearly based around the Austrian Puch design. The engine had two bores of 38mm and a single stroke of 55mm, which put out 7bhp at 5,200rpm. The power unit also included fan-cooling, an inclined cylinder and chain primary drive.

## The Isetta Micro-Car

Next, in 1954, came the famous Isetta micro-car, with its own 236cc overhead-valve air-cooled engine. Originally this was a four-wheeler, with twin narrow-track wheels. Access was by a swing-up front door to which the steering wheel and column were attached. It was produced in a number of countries under licence. The most successful of these was the German BMW marque. Production ceased at ISO in Italy during 1956, but BMW offered the tiny car (often with three wheels) with its own 247cc engine (from its single-cylinder R26/27 motor cycle) until 1963; and from 1957 to 1964 the BMW Isetta was constructed under licence by Isetta of Great Britain Ltd.

The significance of the Isetta to ISO's history cannot be underestimated because the licence agreements provided the funds to develop new vehicles; most notably, as far as this story is concerned, a brand-new scooter design, which made its début in 1957.

## The Diva (Milano)

With enough capital in place, ISO were able to build what is now seen as one of the best of all Italian-made scooters: the Diva (also known as the Milano in certain export markets, including Great Britain), was according to Michael Dregni, 'a masterpiece'. Going on to explain his views:

> Like the TV Lambretta, the Diva was a large-bore luxury scooter designed for touring. The scooter market had grown from basic, boring transportation to buyers with extra cash in their pockets and free time to spend; they wanted a scooter that could take them to the beach on holiday as well as about town. The Lambretta TV, Vespa GS, and the ISO Diva were the scooters of a new Italy.

### *A Cross Between A Vespa and A Lambretta*

The Diva had certain features that made it very popular with buyers: easy accessibility (by simply removing six nuts the entire engine and rear suspension could be exposed for ease of maintenance); a double-capacity battery that meant additional electrical items could be fitted without fear of the system expiring; superb suspension; 10in wheels; an excellent tubular frame; plus a mixture of Vespa and Lambretta styling cues.

As other scooter manufacturers were to discover to their cost, potential buyers could easily be put off by garish styling, unconventional features or even excessive bulk and weight. By largely following the Vespa/Lambretta route, ISO had created a worthy challenger which sold in significant numbers mainly to the home market.

### *On the Technical Front*

The Diva's engine did not follow previous ISO scooter practice; instead, it was a conventional piston-port single-cylinder two-stroke, with square bore and stroke dimensions of 57x57mm. The exact displacement being 146cc, running on a compression ratio of 6.5:1, maximum power was 6bhp at 5,000rpm. There was a four-speed twist-grip-controlled gearbox and multi-plate clutch, whilst chains were employed for both the primary and secondary drive functions. Like most Italian scooters of the period, ignition was by flywheel magneto. Weighing in at 215lb (97.5kg), the Diva could reach 55mph (88km/h). Like the Vespa, the new ISO scooter used single-sided stub axles to support the wheels.

By 1960 the Diva – marketed as the Milano – was being imported into Great Britain by Stuart and Payne Ltd of London.

### Branching Out

For 1961, the Diva was joined by a trio of new overhead-valve four-stroke lightweight motor cycles, two 125s and a 175.

One ISO that did not enter production was a 492cc overhead-valve flat twin-motor cycle displayed in prototype guise at the Milan Samples Fair during April 1961. This featured a full duplex frame, push-button starting, 26bhp and a claimed 90mph (145km/h) performance.

At the end of 1963, all two-wheeled production came to a halt, and ISO went down a totally different route by concentrating upon high-price, luxury cars. These included the Rivolta, which had made its début at the Turin Show late in 1962, and the Grifo.

After several turbulent years of automobile production, ISO was finally declared bankrupt in 1975, having been killed off by the huge increase in oil prices during the mid-1970s. And although a new company using the same brand name resumed production of some cars briefly, things finally ground to a halt again in 1979, this time permanently.

### MV Agusta

The story of *Meccanica Verghera* (MV) Agusta really began as early as 1907, when a wealthy Italian, Giovanni Agusta, became one of the very first of Italy's aviation pioneers. He constructed a simple pusher biplane less than four years after the Wright brothers had achieved the world's first successful powered flight at Kitty Hawk in December 1903.

Subsequently, Giovanni Agusta went on to become a major player in the Italian aircraft industry, but in November 1927, he died prematurely at the age of forty-eight, and the business passed to his wife. The couple had four sons, Domenico, Vincenzo, Mario and Corrado. Domenico, the eldest, soon proved to have a natural flair for the business world. From then until the end of the Second World War, the Agusta family concentrated its energies and production in the aviation sector.

As early as the autumn of 1943, following the deposing of Mussolini, and even though the district around the factory in northern Italy was still under German control, the company began to consider a number of projects aimed at diversifying its activities in a post-war world.

Amongst these projects was a lightweight motor cycle, powered by a 98cc single-cylinder two-stroke engine. As with certain other Italian industrialists, Count Domenico Agusta realized that a ready market would exist for an economical means of transport after the conflict was over. And so, in 1945, MV Agusta was officially formed.

By the time their 98cc motor cycle was ready to begin production, as the Vespa 98, it was late 1945. But, as detailed earlier in this chapter, Piaggio had already registered the Vespa name for its new scooter and therefore MV Agusta was forced to stop using this title.

## MV Agusta Scooters

In a report of the Milan Show in *Motor Cycling* dated 7 December 1950, Cyril Quantrill had this to say regarding the MV Agusta stand; 'Versatility! Two exhibits by the famous racing firm of MV Agusta. The 125cc two-stroke scooter and – a sensation – the road-going version of the renowned 500cc dohc four-cylinder racer.'

In late 1948, with several successful motor cycle models behind him, Count Agusta authorized his engineers to follow the lead set by Vespa, Lambretta and ISO, and design a scooter, the prototype of which appeared early the following year. Called the Model A, it was a production version, and the Model B arrived in 1949. It shared its full monocoque bodywork and single-sided front and rear lug axles with the Vespa design. As for the engine, this had a capacity of 123.5cc (53x56mm), which put out 5bhp at 4,800rpm. Cooling was by fan with a flywheel magneto looking after the ignition; a wet multi-plate clutch operated together with a four-speed transmission; wheel size was 10in, with 3.50 section tyres at front and rear.

During 1950, the Model B was joined by the *Popolare* (popular) scooter, essentially an undressed version at a cheaper price, which looked similar to the early Lambretta series at the rear and the Vespa at the front. Renamed *Normale* in 1951, it was renamed again as the CGT (*C. Gran Turismo*); and from the 1952 model year the CGT was available with a 149cc (58.5x56mm) power unit.

Also in 1950, the Model C replaced the B with a tube-steel chassis covered by unstressed bodywork with similar styling. For the 1951 season, the *C. Super Lusso* (CSL) was offered. A distinctive feature of the CSL was its handlebar-mounted gear-selector indicator. Production came to an end later that year.

## The *Ovunque*

Like the firm's contemporary production motor cycles, the MV Agusta scooters sold well in Italy during the early 1950s, the country still having a huge demand for economical transport. This sales success spurred MV Agusta into designing another scooter. Named the *Ovunque* (everywhere) this was not simply an update of the existing machinery. Instead it was almost a completely new design, although it did employ the familiar CGT engine, but with only three speeds.

*MV Agusta built a whole family of scooters, culminating with the launch in 1960 of the Chicco with a 148cc engine and four-speed gearbox.*

*Another famous Italian motorcycle builder was Moto Guzzi, which launched its Galletto in 1950. Only its 17in wheels defied traditional scooter practice.*

In several other ways the *Ovunque* was ahead of its time, with not only unusual styling, but an innovative single-shock rear suspension, almost identical to the monoshock layout used on high-tech superbikes today.

Leg shields were omitted and there was in fact minimal weather protection for the rider, although extensions of the footboards curved upwards at the front as far as the bottom steering head bearing. The mudguards were now separate assemblies, whilst the fuel tank was positioned behind the seat, the whole effect giving the *Ovunque* a far more stream-lined appearance. The front forks were changed to a leading link design with suspension units on both sides. The wheels were of a similar design, but now carried larger 5.1in (130mm) brake drums and smaller 8in tyres.

By the 1952 model year, the *Ovunque* had totally replaced the CGT on the production lines; it was to remain within the MV Agusta range until late 1954.

**The Pullman**

Both the Type C series and the *Ovunque* proved good sellers. Their success was to lead directly to one of MV Agusta's most popular machines of the 1950s, the Pullman. This was half-scooter, half-motor cycle and was launched at the 1953 Swiss Show. MV Agusta was following directly in the wheelracks of similar devices from Moto Guzzi, Velocette, Motom and ISO.

In common with the *Ovunque*, the Pullman featured a massive single tube frame, passing downwards in front of the engine. However, apart from this feature, the Pullman employed a totally new chassis owing more to conventional motor cycle practice than scooter design, with a swinging arm and twin rear shock absorbers. Telescopic front forks were fitted, with gaiters at the bottom of each leg in a similar fashion to those found on the BSA DI Bantam. A large fuel tank completed the motor cycle side of the specification, whilst the

49

*The Galletto's overhead-valve four-stroke engine; originally 150, then 160, and from 1955, the definitive 192cc displacement that remained until production finally ended in the mid-1960s.*

scooter influence surfaced with footboards for the rider, a single sprung seat, smaller 3.50x15in tyres and a twist-grip hand gear change.

Unlike previous MV Agusta cylinder barrels, however, the one fitted to the Pullman had twin exhaust ports, each of which featured separate exhaust header pipes and silencers on either side of the machine. The barrel (and exhaust layout) were also fitted to the *Ovunque* from 1953 onwards. However, the most technically innovative feature of the Pullman (and *Ovunque*) was the introduction of a separate oil tank with metered lubrication.

### Yet More Scooters
MV Agusta exhibited yet another scooter design in 1953, at the Brussels Show. This was brand-new, but still using a two-stroke engine. However, it never got beyond the prototype stage. Then in the second half of the 1950s, scooter production at MV Agusta's plant lapsed. But right at the very end of the decade in November 1959, MV Agusta revived the concept with two designs, one of which ultimately reached production status. The first, and unsuccessful, entry was a prototype – a 165cc overhead-valve twin-cylinder model. But although it did not enter production, its chassis formed the basis for the 148cc *Chicco* scooter that MV Agusta manufactured and sold from 1960 through to 1964.

### The *Chicco*
Very much in the mould of the bestselling Lambretta Li150, the *Chicco* (grain) looked the most conventional of all the MV Agusta scooters, with its forepeak front mudguard and a neat 4.7in (120mm) Aprilia headlamp carried in a casque-cum-handlebar cover. Its pressed-steel rear enclosure had smooth lines, broken only by the single saddle and rear parcel carrier. The filler cap for a 1.5gal (7ltr) fuel tank was located between the seat and the carrier. Two small inspection covers, one on each side, allowed access to the engine for servicing, and the nearside (left) panel incorporated a toolbox.

Beneath these enclosures was a horizontal single-cylinder, two-stroke engine with piston-port induction, displacing 148cc (57x61mm). This produced 5.8bhp at 5,200rpm, giving the *Chicco* a top speed of 53mph (85km/h). Primary drive was by a simplex chain, with the final drive by duplex chain running in an oil bath case.

The *Chicco's* four-speed gearbox was twist-grip operated, with ignition courtesy of a 6-volt, 30-watt flywheel magneto, whilst a 7-amp hour battery provided power for the parking lights and horn.

A comfortable ride was guaranteed by the hydraulically controlled suspension, pivoted arm rear and trailing link front. The *Chicco's* 3.50x10in tyres were carried on interchange-able split steel rims bolted to 5.9in (150mm) finned aluminium brake hubs, and to change the rear wheel, an additional support stand was supplied in the tool kit. This component was located into the base of the alloy final drive casing to lift the rear wheel clear of the ground, making it a much easier task than with most scooters.

The *Chicco* was updated for the 1962 season by the simple addition of a one-piece dual seat. This (as with the updated Lambretta Li series) transformed the appearance and gave the machine a much more modern style.

Although the *Chicco* was widely exported, including to the USA where it was imported by Cosmopolitan Motors, it, together with the other MV Agusta scooters, whilst interesting, never seriously challenged the Vespa, Lambretta or ISO, on the all-important domestic market.

After production of the *Chicco* ceased in mid-1964, MV Agusta quit the scooter market for good. Today, the aura of the MV Agusta name means that anything with the famous badge sells at premium prices, but in truth there are far more interesting and technically advanced scooters for a more realistic price tag from other manufacturers' ranges.

*Like Piaggio and MV Agusta, Aermacchi came to scooters via the aviation industry. This brochure dates from the early 1950s.*

## Moto Guzzi

In the years immediately following the end of the Second World War, Italy's then-largest motor cycle brand, Moto Guzzi, had enjoyed a boom in sales, in common with the majority of other bike builders. At first, small capacity two-strokes had been the order of the day, either in the form of 'clip-on' engine units that could be fitted to a conventional pedal cycle or a kind of lightweight motor cycle such as Guzzi's own bestselling Motoleggera 65.

However, towards the end of the 1940s, the

*Aermacchi's first try at the two-wheeled game was this prototype electric scooter, circa 1943.*

customer was becoming more affluent and, with this increased prosperity, more demanding in their requirements for choice and specification. Already scooters such as the Vespa and Lambretta had made significant inroads into sales and profits, forcing established motor cycle factories to sit up and notice. This level of success had not gone unnoticed at Moto Guzzi, with the result that they began work in late 1949 on the *Galletto*.

## The *Galletto*

The *Galletto* (cockerel) was neither a scooter nor a motor cycle in the true sense of the word, instead, like the British Velocette LE (*see* Chapter 4), what it represented was what the

traditional motor cycle manufacturer *thought* the potential scooter buyer would want. And although the Moto Guzzi offering was somewhat more successful than the British machine, both were like fleas on the back of a dog when sales figures are compared with those of Vespa or Lambretta.

Even so, the *Galletto* was in many ways an excellent machine for its intended purpose of offering its potential buyer the best of both worlds: the weather protection and the level of comfort and enclosure of a scooter, but the riding position, stability, road holding (thanks to a 17in wheel size) and braking performance of a motor cycle. And like the Velocette, it had the advantage of a four-stroke engine that offered long life and frugal fuel consumption.

Like the British model, which had been launched a few months earlier, its drawbacks were, at least compared with the best scooters, bulk, weight, a higher purchase price and the fact that the Velocette LE and *Galletto* were the first of a kind, so no-one, not even their manufacturers, could gauge how well they would be accepted by the buying public.

The prototype *Galletto* made its public entry on the first day of the Geneva Show on 16 March 1950, where it created a great deal of interest. This first prototype, although essentially the same as the production version that followed, had an engine size of 150cc (61x53mm) and a three-speed gearbox.

By the time series production began later that year, the capacity had grown to 159.5cc (62x53mm). But as with the Velocette LE that had begun life at 149cc and later increased to 192cc, the *Galletto* in its original guise was found to be under powered and was subsequently first increased to 174.4cc (65x53mm) with four speeds in 1952, before being increased again, this time to a definitive 192cc (65x58mm) from 1954, until production finally ended in 1966 (from 1960 an electric start was standard).

The *Galletto's* overhead-valve four-stroke engine (like the LE's) was purpose-built. Even so, it followed Guzzi's time-honoured principle of having a horizontal single cylinder.

*The Aermacchi 125N of 1953 was a strange mixture of scooter and motorcycle components, using a two-stroke engine with a single horizontal cylinder.*

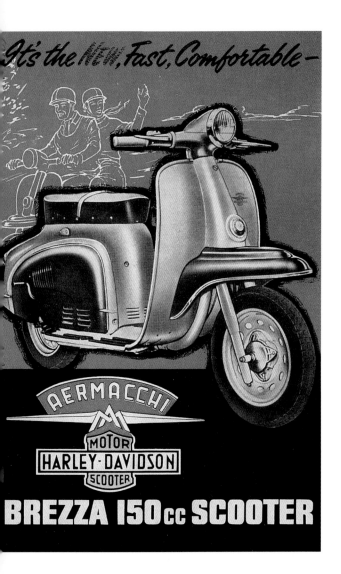

In 1960 Aermacchi joined forces with the American Harley-Davidson company. One of the first fruits of the marriage was a brand-new 148cc scooter, the Brezza, which made its début in 1962.

But if the power unit was familiar to Guzzi fans, the rest of the package was just the reverse.

### Technicalities

Wherever one looked on the *Galletto*, it was possible to find technically interesting features.

For example, unusually, the crankshaft was so designed that in effect it only had a flywheel on the nearside (left). Integral with this was the crankpin that featured a screw-in retainer and pressed-in end gap on the 'exposed' side.

Lubrication was dry sump, with the gear-driven pump housed in the nearside outer crankcase, along with the flywheel magneto, clutch and a train of four helical-drive gears.

*A Rumi mechanic holds one of the horizontally-split 125cc crankcases, which was much easier to work on than the conventional vertically split case.*

*The legendary 124.68cc (42x45mm) Rumi engine was noted for its high performance and turbine-like smoothness.*

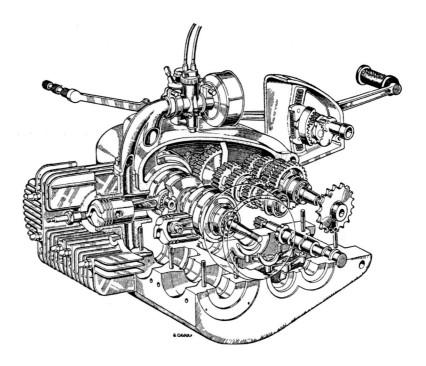

Final drive (in motor cycle fashion) was by exposed chain.

The frame was constructed from a tubular-steel main spar with sheet-metal pressings around the engine, the latter being held in its frame by a series of bolts. This could be removed relatively quickly by dropping it down to the left and rear, whilst the frame was supported by a substantial centre stand (fitted as standard equipment).

Unlike a conventional motor cycle, the frame left a space between the rider's legs – *á la* scooter. The fuel tank was centrally situated behind the rider's leg shields. Front suspension was by leading link forks with fully enclosed suspension units. The rear suspension had the then-unusual feature of a single rear fork that carried the wheel on the right side of the machine. Its movement was controlled by a pair of horizontal coil springs mounted side-by-side in a case above the engine. On the left of this fork the rear wheel was carried, which

was supported by a shaft passing through the brake hub and sprocket, secured by a large castle nut with a washer and split pin.

The wheels were fully interchangeable and were both equipped with 17in tyres. To enable simple tyre changes, the frame incorporated detachable 'jack' legs, and to make life really easy for the *Galletto* rider, a notable feature was a spare wheel as standard equipment, mounted at the front of the rider's leg shields.

The *Galletto* was the nearest Moto Guzzi ever got to a scooter; strange, really, when you consider that the Vespa brand could well have been a Guzzi!

## Aermacchi

Like Piaggio and Agusta, *Aeronautica Macchi* – more simply known as Aermacchi – came to scooters (and motor cycles) from an aviation background. Varese, a small provincial town near the Swiss border, had been a centre for the

## The Rumi *Formichino*

Designed by the former Saroléa and FN engineer Luigi Salmaggi, the new Rumi scooter, the *Formichino* (little ant) caused something of a sensation when it made its public bow at the Milan Spring Fair in April 1954. As scooter enthusiast Mike Webster points out, 'Whilst not the first Rumi scooter, the unorthodox use of alloy castings for its body and mudguards, guaranteed instant attention.'

Its body consisted of four light-alloy castings (manufactured in Rumi's own foundry) held together with Allen bolts, and Rumi's legendary 124cc (42x45mm) air-cooled parallel twin engine with a forward facing horizontal cylinder that was an integral part of the frame structure. So the engine was not, as such, suspended, as many observers initially thought. Incorporated with the frame/body, the headlamp nacelle was joined directly to the fuel tank, immediately below the handlebars.

To the rear of the gearbox a casting encased the final drive chain and doubled as a swinging arm, with rubber rear suspension, whilst the front forks were of the leading link type. The individual saddles were sprung for additional comfort.

*An advertisement from Rumi's British agents during the late 1950s.*

There is no doubt that the widespread use of aluminium in its construction greatly assisted performance, with even the *Normale* (standard) version of the *Formichino* being capable of around 60mph (100km/h), weighing in (dry) at 180lb (81.6kg) thanks to its excellent power-to-weight ratio. Talking of output figures: with a compression ratio of 6.5:1, a single Dell'Orto OAI55 carburettor and a petroil mixture of 20:1; this was 6.5bhp at 6,500rpm. The cylinder barrels were cast-iron in construction, although the heads were light alloy. The four-speed gearbox (by rocking pedal change) was driven through a wet multiplate clutch; the primary drive was by helical gear and the final drive by enclosed chain. The crankcase split horizontally and thus allowed easy maintenance of the gearbox and related components (as the Japanese found years later!).

The Rumi engine, installed integrally with the body, proved wonderfully vibration-free; indeed I have witnessed the famous act of an old English three-penny piece (a 12-sided coin), being placed on the top edge of the crankcase and when the engine was taken up to maximum revolutions there was little or no movement whatsoever!

Thanks to a low centre of gravity, together with excellent weight distribution, the *Formichino* provided superb handling and road holding. But it is worth noting that the original standard model was equipped with 4.00x8 tyres, whereas the Sport version came with 3.50x10: of course this also meant that the latter's wheel diameter was larger and more effective at higher speeds. The brakes on all versions had a diameter of 5in (127mm).

There were, however, some potential draw-

*The Rumi Formichino is seen by many as the definitive sporting scooter, thanks to its superb 125cc horizontal twin-cylinder engine and lightweight aluminium body.*

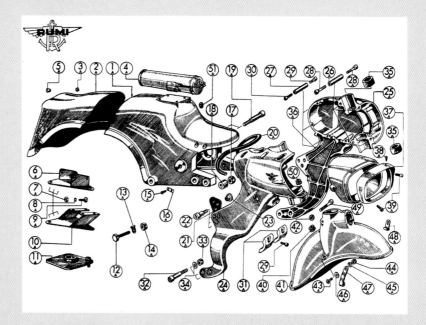

*The unique Rumi aluminium body components.*

backs to what can otherwise be described as a masterpiece. The first concerned the extremely small size of the machine, which put off many taller or larger potential owners. Also, by normal scooter standards, it had minimal weather protection and a quite noisy exhaust. In addition, when new, there was an excessively long-winded running-in procedure (which was essential for future health and performance). A screw, sealed by the dealer, was placed in the top of the carburettor. Any attempt to remove or tamper with it by anyone outside the dealer network invalidated the manufacturer's warranty. Over the initial 2,000 miles (3,200km), the dealer would progressively shorten this screw, thus gradually allowing wider throttle openings.

By the 1958 model year there were no fewer than four *Formichino* models: the 125; the 150 (150cc – 46x45mm); the *Tipo* Sport, with a single 0.9in (23mm) carburettor and a speed of 65mph (104.5km/h); and the E (economy), which had cheaper pressed-steel panel work rather than the cast-alloy bodywork of the other three models.

In 1959 Rumi celebrated its success from 1956–58 in the legendary French *Bol d'Or* 24-hour motor cycle races by introducing its *Bol d'Or* version. In 1956, in the Sports category a *Formichino* ridden by Cambis and Ditail won, at an average speed of 44.34mph (71.3km/h). In 1957, Rumi took the first two places in the racing class, competing against machines of up to 175cc. Then, finally, in 1958 Foidelli and Bois completed a race distance of 1,302 miles

(2,095km) at an average of 54.25mph (87.3km/h) to win the newly introduced 125cc racing class.

The *Bol d'Or* model had a list of high-performance goodies including: chrome-lined aluminium cylinder barrels (made in West Germany by the KS concern); twin 0.7in (18mm) or 0.9in (23mm) Dell'Orto carburettors; a higher compression ratio; and bigger ports. The *Bol d'Or* was only sold in a unique gold and white finish. There was also a sports dual seat and lower handlebars. Rumi claimed 8.5bhp at 7,200rpm and this exciting 125 could reach an impressive 75mph (121km/h).

The first *Formichino's* arrived in Great Britain in November 1955, imported by Scooters & Vehicle Concessionaires of London – who were to remain the sole British importer until Rumi ceased production.

It was also built by Saroléa in Belgium under the name *Dijn* (goblin).

Today, the *Formichino* and in particular the more sporting versions are probably the most sought after and costly of all classic scooters.

| Specification | 1956 Rumi *Formichino* |
|---|---|
| Engine | Air-cooled, horizontal two-stroke, twin |
| Displacement | 124cc |
| Bore & stroke | 42x45mm |
| Gearbox | Four-speed, foot-change |
| Wheel size | 8in (Sport 10in) |
| Power | 6.5bhp |
| Maximum speed | 60mph (96.5km/h) |

*The Scoiattolo was Rumi's first scooter and made its début at the 1951 Milan Show. It used 14in wheels and the famous 125cc horizontal twin-cylinder engine.*

Italian aviation industry since 1912, when the firm of *Nieuport-Macchi*, or to give its correct title, *Societá Anonina-Nieuport-Macchi*, was established there by Giulio Macchi; Nieuport was a French concern that Macchi built his earliest designs with, thanks to a licence agreement.

Soon Aermacchi was turning out its own creations, the most famous of which were its series of Schneider Trophy racing sea-planes culminating in the MC 72. In 1934 an MC 72 set a new world speed record for piston-engined sea-planes at 440.69mph (709km/h), a record that still stands today.

### The First Scooter Appears

After building what are generally accepted to have been Italy's finest fighter aircraft of the Second World War, Aermacchi took its first step towards two-wheeled manufacturing when it constructed a prototype electric scooter in 1943.

Anticipating the post-war boom in affordable transport, Aermacchi bosses looked for a competent designer who could come up with a suitable machine. Their choice was Lino Tonti, who had been at Benelli and had worked during the war on aero-engines.

### The Aermacchi 125

What Tonti came up with was referred to as *Lo scooter trasformable* (the transformable scooter). This was decidedly unorthodox. In some ways it was similar to the Moto Guzzi *Galletto*, in that it was essentially a scooter with motor cycle-size wheels (17in). But unlike the Guzzi, the Aermacchi model was much lighter and powered by a two-stroke engine. This employed full unit construction and featured a horizontal cylinder, together with three speeds. Maximum power was 5bhp at 4,500rpm, giving a top speed of 47mph (76km/h). The frame was of the open type in which the engine pivoted in unit with the rear suspension.

From the original model, simply marketed as the Aermacchi 125, were developed a whole series of variants – the U, M, and N, plus a 250 twin that had smaller 16in wheels, and although it retained a U-shape frame, it was given a conventional motor cycle fuel tank and so cannot really be referred to as a scooter. For interest's sake it is worth noting that the twin also used horizontal cylinders.

### The *Zeffiro*

The 250 twin proved a poor seller and was soon axed. However, the U-frame 125cc Aermacchi two-stroke lightweights continued, the ultimate development being the *Zeffiro* (sapphire) that arrived in the mid-1950s and ran through to the beginning of the next decade. The *Zeffiro* was sold with two engine sizes, 123 and 147.93cc; the increase in displacement was due to a larger bore size of 57mm (from 52mm), the stroke remaining unchanged at 58mm.

Power output of the larger-engined model was 8.5bhp at 5,500rpm (against 6.5bhp at the same revolutions). Like its smaller brother, the 150 *Zeffiro* continued the familiar Aermacchi

*The famous motorcycle racing marque FB Mondial presented its new 160cc scooter at the Milan Show in January 1952.*

trademark of a horizontal cylinder and, as on the 125 version, a three-speed twist-grip-operated gearbox. But there were notable differences between the two: the bigger model having a redesigned and sturdier frame, with revised rear suspension and a dual seat assembly.

There was even a *Motocarro* (motor cycle truck). This employed the front end of the 150 *Zeffiro*, including not only the engine assembly but also some of the cycle parts such as the front forks, front mudguard and leg shield assembly, to make up an entirely new rear half – the truck section. As with the two-wheeled

*Zeffiro*, the engine was fan-cooled and a kick-starter was used to bring it to life.

It is worth pointing out that very many other scooter manufacturers, including Vespa, Lambretta and Ducati, offered similar three-wheeled vehicles.

### The *Brezza*

In 1960, Aermacchi was split into two. The two-wheeled division was partnered with Harley-Davidson, the aviation arm going to Lockheed. In 1962 a brand-new scooter, the *Brezza* (breeze) was introduced. The newcomer was very much in the traditional

Although founded as long ago as 1926, Ducati did not begin production of powered two-wheelers until after the Second World War – and then this was for the auxiliary 'clip-on' engine, named the *Cucciolo* (little pup).

The *Cucciolo* proved a major commercial success; first simply as the engine assembly referred to above and, as the 1940s gave way to the 1950s, as the basis for a line of lightweight motor cycles and mopeds of 49, 60 and 65cc.

The *Cucciolo* also had the effect of convincing Ducati's management that two-wheelers were where the Bologna firm's future lay and therefore, at the 1952 Milan Show, two brand-new machines made their bow, a 98cc ohv motor cycle and a scooter.

Ducati had seen the tremendous success achieved by Piaggio's Vespa and Innocenti's Lambretta machines. However, Ducati's offering was completely different. This is how Michael and Eric Dregni described it in their *Motor Scooter Buyer's Guide* (Motorbooks, 1993): 'The

Cruiser was stylish, like a metallic sharkskin suit on wheels. Its step-through chassing was clothed in elegant, flowing two-tone bodywork penned and produced by the celebrated Italian *Carrozzeria*, Ghia.'

But if Ducati thought it could steal the thunder from the likes of Vespa and Lambretta, which by then were streaming off production lines throughout Italy, it was to be mistaken.

Ducati's design was in fact totally different from mainstream scooter thought – not only was it a four-stroke, but powerful – the engine had to be detuned to meet Italian legislation governing scooters at that time. The best comparison is to think of the Cruiser as an Aston Martin or Porsche, whereas the Vespas and Lambrettas were the Ford or Volkswagen products.

The Cruiser's engine displaced 175cc, with bore and stroke dimensions of 62x58mm. At first the power output was in excess of 12bhp – a class-leading figure at that time, but this had to

*The Cruiser was an impressive sight and the centre of attention at the International Milan Show that opened on 12 January 1952.*

*With a 175cc engine, automatic transmission and an innovative electric start, plus styling by Ghia, the 1952 Cruiser should have been a big sales success – in reality it was just the opposite.*

be cut down to a restricted 8bhp, due to the government ruling referred to above. This power cut resulted in the Cruiser having too much flab and not enough muscle. In its detuned state, the compression ratio had been reduced to 7.5:1 and maximum engine revolutions dropped to 6,000.

Even so, the Ducati Cruiser was an innovative, technically interesting machine and is today seen as the Rolls-Royce of the scooter world. Its most noteworthy feature was its automatic transmission, this being in the form of a hydraulic torque converter, the principal being similar to that employed by Moto Guzzi on its V1000 Convert de Luxe touring motor cycle of the 1970s. The torque converter assembly was bolted to the horizontally disposed engine via an aluminium casting that incorporated the swinging arm pivot. The gearbox ran lengthways under the rear bodywork, driving the rear wheel via a short connecting shaft to a crown wheel and pinion. Both front and rear suspension was by way of a single hydraulic unit and the 10in wheels were shod with 3.50-section, white-walled tyres.

Another innovative feature of the Cruiser was its electric start (using a massive 30-amp, 6-volt battery), the first to be employed on a scooter anywhere in the world.

Other features included sprung separate seats for the rider and pillion passenger, a built-in headlight with a large grill below it, and hinged side panels to allow access for maintenance purposes. A spare wheel was carried under the left-hand panel, with the battery positioned centrally above the engine assembly.

However, although without doubt the most technically advanced scooter of its era,

the Cruiser unfortunately proved to be a resounding sales flop. This was for several reasons: its complex specification; poor performance and acceleration – the maximum speed was only 50mph (80km/h); it was heavy and costly to manufacture and expensive to buy. Hence it was only manufactured for some two years, during which a mere 2,000 were produced.

The lesson of the Cruiser's failure had been a bitter one – and Ducati did not re-enter the scooter field until the mid-1960s (this time with cheap-to-buy 50 and 100cc two-stroke models). However, the Italian industry generally kept to the Vespa/Lambretta formula and only the Germans, and to a lesser extent the British, entered the top end of the market that the Cruiser had been intended for.

| Specification | 1952 Ducati Cruiser |
|---|---|
| Engine | Fan-cooled, ohv, single |
| Displacement | 175cc |
| Bore & stroke | 62x58mm |
| Gearbox | Automatic |
| Wheel size | 10in |
| Power | 8bhp |
| Maximum speed | 55mph (88km/h) |

*Cover from the now 'rare as hen's teeth' Cruiser Owner's Handbook.*

scooter mould with small wheels (12in) and a comprehensive enclosure as found, for example, on the Vespa.

With its much more modern design and style, the *Brezza* was intended to replace the *Zeffiro*. However, in reality it came too late, as scooter sales were already on the slide all over Europe.

The 147.93cc (57x58mm) fan-cooled piston – port single-cylinder two-stroke

engine – retained the horizontal cylinder layout, but otherwise the *Brezza* represented a major change of direction from earlier Aermacchi scooters.

## Rumi, The Prestige Marque

Rumi enjoys a unique place in the history of the scooter. And its definitive product, the *Formichino* (little ant) is one of the very few scooters that is respected by motor cycle enthusiasts. Certainly, when I was editor of *Motor Cycle Enthusiast* magazine during the 1980s, the mere mention of the Rumi name inspired favourable comments from readers in a way that only a true classic can.

*Officine Fonderie Rumi* was founded by Donnino Rumi in Bergamo, just prior to the outbreak of the First World War. During the 1920s the company manufactured cast components for the textile machine industry and, very soon afterwards, complete machines. By the early 1930s Rumi had acquired an enviable reputation for both design and quality within the textile industry.

During the Second World War, Rumi became involved in an entirely different engineering field, the construction of midget two-man submarines and torpedoes. With the conflict at an end there was obviously a dearth of contracts for any form of armaments, so Rumi looked at other ways of keeping their production facilities active. Besides general engineering, a decision was taken to diversify into motor cycles, which were then enjoying a sales boom.

*Besides its earlier expensive failure with the four-stroke Cruiser in the 1950s, Ducati also built a range of lightweight scooters from the mid-1960s with 48 and 94cc two-stroke engines. This is the Brio 100 of 1966.*

### Production Begins

The first Rumi, the 125 Turismo motor cycle made its début at the Milan Spring Fair in April 1950. At its centre was a 180-degree crankshaft, two-stroke with twin horizontal cylinders. And this advanced power unit was to characterize the marque throughout its twelve-year reign as a prestige motor cycle and

# DUCATI
## 50 ∗ 100

*A Ducati brochure advertising its scooters and mopeds, circa mid-1960s.*

scooter manufacturer. The famous 'Anchor' logo reflected the recent nautical past of the company.

The Rumi engine, employing 42x45mm bore and stroke dimensions, gave a displacement of 124.68cc and provided smooth, almost turbine-like performance.

As Michael Dregni noted:

Rumi motor cycles and scooters were always unique. The engineering was avant garde and innovative; the styling was unlike any other two-wheelers. The features were created by a different mindset – unorthodox frames and forks, handy clocks mounted on gas tanks, odd fittings often individually stamped with Rumi's logo. The Rumi motor scooter was a totally unique creation

**Motorscooter PARILLA "LEVRIERE"**

**153 cc. - two-stroke**

compared to the Vespa, ISO, or Lambretta of the day.

### The *Scoiattolo*

Rumi's first scooter the *Scoiattolo* (squirrel) was introduced at the Milan Show in 1951. It has to be said that when compared with the definitive Rumi scooter, the *Formichino*, the *Scoiattolo* was vastly inferior. It still had the same brilliant engine, but was in many ways a failure as it lacked the compactness, power-to-weight ratio and sheer efficiency of the Vespa.

Like the Vespa, the chassis and bodywork were a steel-stamped assembly without a conventional frame. But with larger 14in wheels and a bulky appearance, the *Scoiattolo* suffered an identity crisis.

Strangely, even after the much superior *Formichino* was launched in 1953, Rumi

continued production of the model until as late as 1957. At first it had only three speeds, but in 1953 an additional ratio was added together with the option of an electric start, which was operated by a pair of 6-volt batteries running in parallel and mounted beneath the larger dual seat assembly. In the same year, an aluminium-bodied sidecar for the *Scoiattolo* was also first offered, this featuring a 3.25x14in wheel. All *Scoiattolo's* produced came with wire wheels.

### The *Formichino*

The *Formichino* was a masterpiece of design and engineering. Utilizing the firm's 125cc horizontal engine and a cast-aluminium chassis together with low weight and a small profile, many versions could reach 65mph (104.5km/h). The model was some 25 per cent quicker than rival marques' 125s – and faster even than most 150cc models. Certainly in racing events the *Formichino* was virtually untouchable in its class – with victory in the prestigious French *Bol d'Or* 24-hour race on more than one occasion.

The *Formichino* was offered over the years in a number of guises: *Normale, Lusso,* Sport, *Economico* and *Bol d'Or.*

## V-Twin Prototypes

In April 1960, Rumi announced a brand-new range of scooters and motor cycles powered by a modular engine concept in three capacities – 98, 125 and 175cc. Two of these engine sizes were displayed in prototype form at that month's Milan Spring Fair, where they attracted great interest.

Whilst the running gear of the motor cycle was similar to that of the then-current motor cycle, the scooter's lines were far more conventional than those of the revolutionary, but expensive to manufacture, *Formichino,* and were something of a cross between a Vespa and a Lambretta.

What really startled observers was the engine/gearbox units, these being superbly crafted miniature ninety-degree v-twins, with pushrod-operated valves and matt-finished engine casings. Oil was contained in a finned sump cast integrally with the crankcase and circulated by a gear-type pump to the main and big-end bearings and the valve gear. Like Ducati's later Vees, the ninety-degree configuration was chosen because this provided optimum balance, thus virtually eliminating vibration.

The larger 173.62cc (48x48mm) engine put out a claimed 8.2bhp and maximum speed (again claimed) was 71mph (114km/h).

As before, the new scooters shared the same power unit as the motor cycles. Starting was again by kick (on the nearside), but gear selection was now by twist-grip on the left handlebar. Attractively styled, the bodywork

and weather shield, with integral front mudguard, were formed from sheet-metal pressings with side panels to provide access to the engine. Front suspension was by leading link fork, whilst a pivoted fork was employed at the rear. The 10in diameter pressed-steel split-rims were fitted with 3.50 section tyres.

However, no production of the v-twins was ever undertaken, as shortly afterwards, except for the Junior Gentleman 125cc motor cycle that continued until 1962, Rumi quit vehicle production.

Instead, it returned to military contract work, although Rumi did build a 125cc kart racing engine (the Rocket) from 1960 until 1966. However, this was a single with a vertical cylinder. And then in 1967, Stefano Rumi, son of the founder, built a special 125 model for motorcycle trials using a modified kart engine. But as far as its magnificent *Formichino* scooter is concerned, this was now only history.

## The Scooters' Success Story

In December 1950 *Motor Cycle* published a comprehensive report on the Milan Show. And the following are the reasons it saw at that time for the Italian scooter's huge sales success story on its home market:

> The factors which have caused their great popularity in Italy can be summed up as: elegance; convenience, public transport in Italian towns being a nightmare; extreme economy – 140mpg [2ltr/100km]; cleanliness; remarkable reliability – to see a Vespa or Lambretta broken-down is about as common as the sight of a dead donkey; and such conveniences as an easily changed spare wheel (both machines have stub axles front and rear) and the possibility of carrying the whole family in one way or another, even sidecars being not uncommon appendages.

The *Motor Cycle* report also pointed out other reasons including:

*An August 1964
advertisement for
Cosmopolitan
Motors, the
American importer
for several Italian
marques, notably the
Agrati-built Capri
scooter range.*

OPPOSITE PAGE: *Laverda, famous for its large-capacity
superbikes of the 1970s also built lightweight motorcycles and
this miniscooter, which was available with either a 49 or 60cc
overhead-valve engine during the early 1960s.*

# MINISCOOTER 49-60 cc.

**ENGINE**
Four stroke overhead valve.

**Cylinder head:** Light alloy with inserted cast iron combustion chamber.

**Cylinder:** Light alloy with inserted barrel made of special cast iron.

**49 cc**
**Stroke:** 39 mm.
**Bore** : 40 mm.
**Total piston displacement:** 48.984 c. cms.
**Compression ratio:** 1 : 8
**Horse power output:** 2.5 B.H.P. at 6000 r.p.m.

**60 cc**
**Stroke:** 39 mm.
**Bore** : 47 mm.
**Total piston displacement:** 59.032 c. cms.
**Compression ratio:** 1 : 8
**Horse power output:** 3 B.H.P. at 6000 r.p.m.

**IGNITION**
The ignition process is effected by a flywheel magneto with a contact breaker incorporated accessible from outside. H.T. coil (external).

**FEEDING**
Gravity feed - Fuel tank capacity: 5 litres - 1 imperial gallon.

**Clutch:** Single plate cone clutch in oil bath.

**Gearbox:** 3 speeds. Twist grip control.

**Performance:** 49 cc - Maximum speed 57 Km/h - 35 m.p.h.

60 cc - Maximum speed: 65 Km/h - 40 m.p.h.

Maximum gradient: 20%.

Fuel consumption (C.U.N.A. Regulations) 100 kms per litre 1.6 - 176 miles per gallon.

**FRAME**
Stamped plate frame with rear bearing body.

**Suspension:** Front and rear spring suspension.

**Wheels:** Both wheels are interchangeable and have a detachable spindle.

**Tyre size:** 2.75 x 9.

**Brakes:** Single expanding shoe brake with cable operated control.

The front brake is connected to a hand lever on the right section of the handlebar. The rear brake is connected to a pedal situated on the R. H. side of the scooter.

**Electric equipment:** 6-volt 19-vatt Flywheel alternator.

One advantage which they have hitherto enjoyed, immunity from all formalities of registration and taxation, expires at the end of this year, for all motor scooters have now to be registered. This does not, in Italy, involve third-party insurance, but does involve presenting the vehicle physically for a technical examination to see that it is in sound and roadworthy condition and conforms with the law as to lights, brakes, and so on.

Besides the marques I have covered so far, by the end of 1950 other Italian scooter producers were: Vittoria, Doniselli, Bambi, Orix, San Cristoforo and FM.

## The 1952 Milan Show

When the 29th Milan Show opened on 12 January 1952, the atmosphere was one of unbridled enthusiasm, this coming after registrations of 1,112,500 powered two-wheelers for 1951 – more than 400,000 more than the 1950 figure.

All classes of machine showed substantial increases in numbers, but the biggest total increase was in scooters and lightweight motor cycles, which for 1951 totalled 570,000, against 306,900 for 1950. It was generally agreed that the highlight of this vast exhibition was the brand-new Ducati Cruiser de Luxe scooter with a 175cc ohv engine, electric starter and torque converter transmission.

An electric starter was also standard equipment on another scooter new to the show, from 125cc motor cycle road racing champions FB Mondial. This featured a 160cc two-stroke engine with a four-speed gearbox in the unit. Symmetrical, pear-shape crankcase covers that enclosed the primary transmission, generator and starter motor extended to the rear and formed the fork for the wheel. Hence the engine, the transmission and the wheels were a sub-assembly pivoting under control of two hydraulically operated units.

The duplex frame was made up of tubes welded at the joints, whilst steel pressings were employed for the weather shield, floor and front guard; wheel size was 12in.

## Parilla

The founder, Giovanni Parrilla (the second 'r' being dropped from the trading title) had begun trading in the mid-1940s in Milan, specializing in the repair of agricultural diesel injectors and pumps.

Then, in October 1946, he introduced an overhead-camshaft, 250 single-cylinder racer, which was also sold in super sport form for fast road use. This design was followed by other motor cycles with both four and two-stroke engines. Then came the *Levriere*.

### The *Levriere*

The Milan Show of January 1952 was the setting for the launch of Parilla's *Levriere* (greyhound) scooter, which although not the prettiest example of small wheel art form, was nonetheless a practical and reliable machine, which was ultimately to prove something of a money-spinner for the company. Not only was it built in considerable numbers by Parilla itself, but it was either licensed or imitated by several others, notably Husqvarna (with Swedish HVA engines), the German Victoria Peggy and as a design influence for Zündapp's Bella. It was also widely exported throughout mainland Europe, to Great Britain, the USA and even the Far East, including Vietnam.

But although a commercial success, it only really came about because Parrilla saw the scooter project as a way of funding his more exotic motor cycles.

*Design Features*
The *Levriere* originally came with a 125cc (54x54mm) engine, a three-speed gearbox and twist-grip change. However, from 1953 onwards, a larger 153cc (60x54mm) version

with four speeds and foot-change by rocking pedal was offered.

Both examples featured a central duplex frame covered by sheet-metal bodywork. This bodywork was used not only to protect the rider (which it did really well) from the engine and road grime, but also for aerodynamic purposes. In addition, the central step-through section funnelled cooling air from behind the front wheel rearwards to the engine and transmission, and then out through side vents.

This is what *Motor Cycle* said of the 153cc-powered *Levriere* in a road test published in its 7 April 1955 issue:

> Steering and stability of the Parilla were first class. The model could be ridden feet-up almost to a stand still. Straight-ahead steering was light and positive and steady at all speeds of which the machine was capable … On fast corners the steering had a most satisfactory tank feeling and the machine could be heeled over stylishly.

The 12in wheels were laced to Boranni alloy rims, with 4in (102mm) drum brakes front and rear. Motor cycle influence showed with the suspension layout – telescopic forks at the front and a twin shock swinging arm at the rear. Primary drive was by helical gears, final drive by chain.

All in all, the *Levriere* was a thoroughly competent design, but it lacked the sheer style of the Vespa and, to a lesser extent, the Lambretta models of the period, and was discontinued in 1959.

Parilla built another scooter, but only in prototype form, called the Oscar. However this highly interesting machine (with up-to-date styling and a brand-new 160cc twin-cylinder engine and electric start) came at a bad time for the company. Shortly afterwards, Giovanni Parrilla was forced to sell out to a holding company, SIL, to avoid bankruptcy. And although Parilla motor cycles were still available until as late as 1967 in the USA (after the

*Bianchi's first scooter arrived in April 1960 as the 71.5cc Bi Bi. However, later that year it was replaced by the 80cc Orsetto. Air ducts in the front mudguard were there to assist engine cooling.*

importer purchased the factory's stock in 1963), it was the end of the Parilla scooter line.

## Motobi

In 1949, Giuseppe Benelli began work on a motor cycle known simply as the B. This original model made its début at the Milan Spring Fair in April 1950.

In 1954 the monogram B was axed in favour of the Motobi brand name. And, in November 1956, Motobi displayed a scooter prototype at the Milan Show. This employed a tube frame covered by sheet-steel bodywork. During 1957, Motobi began production of a family of scooters based on the prototype, all using 12in

*In 1961, moped specialists Malaguti built this Lambretta-like Saigon 48cc scooter with a three-speed twistgrip-controlled gearbox.*

wheels. These were the two-stroke *Ardizio*, in 125 and 150cc engine sizes; the four-stroke *Imperiale* with a 125cc ohv engine; and the *Catria* – the top of the range model with a 175cc ohv engine developing 11bhp. The *Catria* was particularly stylish, in a similar mode to Lambretta's LD, with two separate saddles and full bodywork. The official Motobi *Catria* brochure referred to the model as *Lo Scooter per l'intenditore* (the scooter for the one who understood).

Later, from 1959, Motobi introduced a series of scooter-moped type machines with engine sizes up to 125cc. These were produced until the late 1960s.

## Agrati-Garelli

The Agrati-Garelli group was created in 1961, from Agrati, an old-established engineering company, and the famous Garelli motor cycle marque, a major pre-war manufacturer, and during the late 1940s and early 1950s the manufacturer of the ubiquitous Mosquito

'clip-on' auxiliary engine for fitting to bicycles.

Back in 1958, Agrati had introduced its Capri scooter, which Michael Dregni described as a 'brilliant yet simple idea; build a single scooter and equip it with a series of engines and gearboxes to create a complete line to satisfy all markets'. And so, Capris were manufactured with the following engine options: 50cc (3.3bhp) and three speeds; 50cc (4.3bhp) and four speeds; 70cc (3.3bhp) and three speeds; 80cc (4bhp) and three speeds; 125cc (5.5bhp) and four speeds; and 148cc (5.6bhp) and four speeds.

After the 1961 merger, Agrati produced the 98cc Capri, whilst Garelli offered the 125cc Capri de Luxe. There was also another model, this time a totally different design called the Como, but this was only manufactured as a 50cc machine.

Although the Capri range found it tough going on the home Italian market, which was dominated by Vespa and Lambretta, it found its niche as an export success, being sold all around the world, notably in mainland Europe, Great Britain and the USA. Whereas most late-comers to the scooter market were failures both in Italy and abroad, the Capri range bucked that trend. The British importers, Capri Scooters, based Nottingham, began importing the line in November 1959.

## Laverda

Breganze lies in the shadows of the Dolomite mountains in north-east Italy, and is only an hour's swift motoring from Venice. It was also the home of Laverda, a marque that even today stirs passions with lovers of high-performance Italian motor cycles, having been responsible for classics such as the SFC and Toto during the 1970s. But during the 1950s and 1960s Laverda, like the majority of other Italian bike builders, produced lightweight commuter motor cycles and scooters.

### The Miniscooter

The Miniscooter first appeared at the Milan Show in late 1959, and came in direct response to the no tax, no driving licence rule for low-performance two-wheelers that had led to a crop of new tiny scooters.

*Motor Cycle's* Milan Show report explained: 'Among the smaller scooters are two which scorn the proprietary frame pressing. They are the 49cc [40x39mm] ohv Laverda – aimed specifically at the no-tax market – and the Paglianti … The canary-coloured Laverda is extraordinarily chic and features many novelties.'

Actually, the Laverda Miniscooter was offered in two engine sizes. One, mainly for the export market, displaced 59cc (47x39mm). Otherwise both machines were identical. The larger model arrived in 1962 and, together with the original 49cc version, was given three speeds.

Of course a four-stroke for such small engines sizes was almost unique in the scooter world when the Miniscooter was launched.

The engine featured fan-cooling, whilst a 6-volt flywheel magneto supplied current for ignition and direct lighting. The gearbox was operated by twist-grip and a single-plate clutch ran in oil. Final drive was by chain, and tyre size was 2.50x19. Supporting the saddle, a 1gal (4.5ltr) fuel tank hinged up from the main body pressings to provide access to the oil filter and dipstick, sparking plug and carburettor. A remote float tickler protruded through the top of the tank and the fuel tap through the front of the body. Three rubber mats lined the floor, the middle mat covering the tool compartment.

Designed by Laverda engineer Luciano Zen, the Miniscooter never sold in large numbers, even though a similar machine from Vespa – the *Vespino* (that arrived in 1962), albeit with a two-stroke engine, was manufactured in vast quantities. The larger-engined version was also built under licence from 1962 to 1965 by the Spanish Montesa factory, which called it the Micro.

## Bianchi

Bianchi was another famous Italian motor cycle manufacturer that jumped on the lightweight scooter bandwagon. Its first offering came a few months after the Laverda model and was presented for the first time at the Milan Fair in April 1960.

It was a neat lightweight, powered by a 71.5cc two-stroke engine with a horizontal cylinder producing a claimed 3bhp via a three-speed gearbox built-in unit and twist-grip control. Called the Bi Bi, Bianchi's new scooter also featured geared primary drive linked with a multi-plate oil-bathed clutch transmitting power to the rear wheel via a totally enclosed chain on the nearside (left) of the machine.

Air ducts integral with the front mudguard helped cool the engine, which breathed through a 0.6in (15mm) carburettor. Suspension was by telescopic fork at the front, with a swinging arm at the rear. The tyre size was 8in.

In 1960, the Bi Bi was replaced by the 80cc (48x43mm) *Orsetto* (bear cub), with power output increased to 4.5bhp.

## Other Additions To
## The Scooter Ranks

Other manufacturers included Malaguti and Guizzo (both 1961) and Gilera in 1962, plus scooterettes from the likes of Peripoli and Cimatti.

Malaguti produced a pukka scooter, but sporting a 50cc engine, with the name Saigon.

In contrast, the Guizzo was an entirely new de luxe design, described by *Motor Cycle* as 'the Rolls-Royce of Scooters'. The magazine went on to say, 'Certainly the model carries the stamp of quality though whether it will prove sufficiently eyeable for Italian taste may be open to question.' The Guizzo was big – almost as large in front as the German Maicoletta (*see* Chapter 3). Sadly, Guizzo, formerly a moped manufacturer, had misjudged the market and sales never lived up to expectations. This, combined with the costs of developing its scooter, saw the company go bankrupt not long afterwards.

Like Laverda, another famous motor cycle brand, Gilera, chose to go down the four-stroke route when it launched its scooter in spring 1962. And as scooter buff Michael Dregni pointed out, 'Gilera offered its G50 scooter based on bodywork and engine designs that were so similar to the Vespa it is surprising the scooters did not end up doing battle in court instead of in the marketplace.'

However, the G50 did offer certain differences – advantages even – over the 50cc Vespino, which also made its début in 1962. The layout of the Gilera engine was virtually identical to the Piaggio design. But there were two major differences: it was a four-stroke unit with overhead-valves and it was mounted on the other side of the scooter.

Displacing 50cc (38x44mm), it created 1.5bhp at 4,800rpm via three speeds. Later, an 80cc version (coded G80) was offered with increased bore and stroke to the square dimensions of 46x46mm, the bigger unit putting out 3.65bhp at 6,000rpm. The 50cc version had a single seat; the 80cc model, a dual assembly. Both remained in production until 1966, but never sold in large quantities.

## The Decline Sets In

During the late 1960s and early 1970s, scooter sales plummeted and this applied to Italy as well as other countries. Many manufacturers had already disappeared and this trend continued. By the mid-1970s, the only mass-produced scooter left in Italy was the Vespa. In the country that had invented the mass-market scooter, transport needs were changing rapidly as the population became ever more affluent, and the trend moved away from the scooter towards the small, cheap car.

## Scooter Production in Spain

Compared with its Latin neighbour Italy, Spain's contribution to the scooter world was small. During Franco's reign, scooters and motor cycles were not allowed to be imported, so both Lambretta and Vespa models were built in Spain under licence agreements, the same applying to the Agrati Capri.

During the early 1970s, when Innocenti ceased producing Lambrettas in Italy, Spanish versions were then built by Servetta, but generally referred to, at least in export markets, as Lambrettas.

Montesa also built Laverda scooters between 1962 and 1965.

During the period covered by this book, there were only three Spanish producers who combined motor cycle and scooter manufacture: Rieju, Derbi and Montesa.

## Rieju

Rieju is one of Spain's oldest and certainly longest-lived motor cycle manufacturers and is still in business today. Founded in 1952, it began by building an interesting selection of motor cycles with both two- and four-stroke engines, including bought-in French 125 and 174cc ohv power units.

The firm also produced a small number of scooter models, these having motor cycle size wheels and styling akin to the German DKW Hobby (*see* Chapter 3).

## Derbi

Like Rieju, Derbi has a long history of motor cycle manufacture and is still going strong at the beginning of the 21st century. The story began back in 1922, when Simeon Rabasa Singla opened a small workshop for the repair and hire of pedal cycles in the village of Mollet near Barcelona, and from these humble beginnings emerged what was to become an internationally successful marque.

First, Singla moved into the manufacture of pedal cycles, and then in the immediate post-

*Rieju built a scooter and a lightweight motorcycle during the 1950s; both used a horizontal single-cylinder two-stroke engine with three-speed gearbox; wheel size was 16in.*

war period he began motor cycle production, trading under the name of SRS (his initials).

By 1953, with a name change from SRS to Derbi, the company introduced a scooter, the *Masculino* (machismo), the first version of which featured a 98cc single-cylinder two-stroke engine developed from the Model 95 motor cycle.

From 1955, until scooter manufacture ceased in the late 1950s, Derbi also offered a 125 *Masculino*. This had a 123.67cc power unit and was again a single-cylinder two-stroke, based on the 98cc version, but with square bore and stroke dimensions of 54x54mm. Although the engine had also been improved, the 125 unit still retained the original three-speed gearbox, but peak power had increased from 4bhp to 5.2bhp.

However, from this time until 1982, Derbi concentrated on motor cycles and mopeds, rather than scooters.

## Montesa

Founded by Pedro Permanyer and Francisco Bulto, Montesa began motor cycle production in the mid-1940s, and by early 1958 Montesa had built an enviable reputation in both series production and racing. And it was the latter that was to cause Bulto to quit and form his own marque, Bultaco, because Permanyer felt Montesa should save money by not racing.

Shortly after the split, Montesa launched its first scooter at the Geneva Show in March 1958. And it was certainly unconventional. The Montesa scooter dispensed with a conventional frame; instead, its functions were performed by a smooth, stress-bearing body that was manufactured of $^1/_{32}$ in thick steel sheeting and incorporated rubber-lined footboards and a weather shield. Because of difficulties in obtaining satisfactory deep pressings in Spain, rolling was employed to form the body members, which were then welded together. This reduced tooling costs, but the

*The Montesa Micro was in fact a licence-built Italian Laverda. Its four-stroke 49cc engine produced 1.6bhp and could reach 29mph (47km/h).*

appearance suffered as a result of the restriction to single-plane curves.

Of tunnel shape, the middle portion of the body had a flat base and was strengthened by four transverse, channel-section ribs, spot-welded to the inner surface. A tubular cradle carried the engine, gearbox and rear wheel, and was pivoted on a spindle supported in the sides of the body. Withdrawal of the spindle and disconnection of the cradle from the lower ends of the rear shock absorbers permitted the entire unit to be removed for servicing. Normal access to the carburettor, spark plug and clutch adjustment was via side doors.

Built onto full-width brake hubs, the quickly detachable wheels were of 12in diameter and equipped with 3.00 section tyres.

Between the steering head and the weather shield was a plastic fuel tank of 3gal (14ltr) capacity, on top of which was a facia containing the filler cap, speedometer, ignition warning light and ignition key holder. A 12-volt starter-generator was mounted on the crankshaft of the 142cc single-cylinder engine. Montesa sources claimed a maximum speed of 50mph (80km/h).

The seats and standard-fitment luggage rack were mounted on rails and could thus be adjusted fore and aft.

But lacking many features buyers demanded from a more conventional scooter, the Montesa effort was not a success and production was halted at the end of 1959.

From 1962 onwards, Montesa built the Italian Laverda Miniscooter, as the Micro Scooter. With its 49 or 60cc four-stroke engine, it was the sole four-stroke that Montesa ever built. From 1966 through to the end of production this tiny scooter was renamed the Micro 66.

From then, until the 1980s, the Spanish industry concentrated upon motor cycles rather than scooters.

# 3   West Germany and Austria

*Hoffman began building the Vespa scooter under licence from Piaggio in late 1949.*

Compared with countries such as Italy, Great Britain and the USA, Germany was slow to resume post-war production during the late 1940s. This was largely due to the country being split into zones of occupation, which saw the east come under Soviet control. The western powers (the USA, Great Britain and France) then proposed the creation of a separate West German state, the first constitutional bodies of the new Federal Republic being formed in September 1949, with its capital in Bonn. The following month, the Soviets proclaimed their occupied zone a state, calling it the German Democratic Republic, with its seat of power in the eastern sector of Berlin.

This chapter will deal with scooters manufactured in West Germany; those produced in the east are to be found in Chapter 7.

## The 1950 Frankfurt Show

The first of its kind since the Second World War, the Frankfurt Show (for two and three-wheeled vehicles) took place in March 1950, and in effect signalled the beginning of the post-war West German scooter industry.

As *Motor Cycle* dated 30 March 1950 reported, 'The surprises of the Show centre around scooters. A big publicity campaign has heralded the NSU Lambretta … Another Italian scooter which is to be seen on German roads is the Vespa, which is produced under licence by Hoffman.'

As for original West German designs, there was the Till, which was being produced by

Riedel (manufacturers of the unique Imme motor cycle). Göricke also displayed a scooter, powered by a 98cc Ilo two-stroke engine. As the *Motor Cycle* Frankfurt Show report remarked, 'In the past [post-war], German manufacturers have catered for the low-price market with very small motor cycles or cycle attachments. To offer scooters is really a departure from tradition.'

## A Decade of Progress

The arrival of the scooter in West Germany was to mark the beginning of a new phase where the industry was to rise from the ashes of the Second World War to a position that by the mid-1950s was the envy of the two-wheeled world, but then was to virtually disappear by the end of that decade.

From 1945 until the end of 1949, there had only been a simple requirement for cheap utility machines. Then in the early 1950s, the accent switched to technical innovation, performance and luxury – clearly showing the vast improvement in living standards. By the mid-1950s the West German economic miracle was in full swing.

As a result, the requirements of the West German user switched from two to four wheels, even though for a period of time this was masked by large sales of scooters (and micro-cars).

Initially, a high level of road taxation and insurance rates for cars, plus the high price of petrol in West Germany, increased the ranks of motorcyclists and scooterists. Many professionals including doctors, lawyers and businessmen, who in other European countries

*NSU constructed its versions of the Lambretta in West Germany from 1950 until 1956, when it began to produce its own designs.*

or the USA would have normally used a car, in West Germany rode a motor cycle or scooter.

This led to an unparalled rush by manufacturers to build ever more technically advanced and luxurious scooters. All this created a false sense of well-being in the West German scooter industry. Many companies overextended themselves in the headlong stampede to produce new, more complex (and expensive) models. But by the time these appeared in 1955–56, the market was dwindling as potential buyers melted away to purchase their first cars, which explains why so many West German scooters were exported – and why their design, construction and quality were so outstanding. If Italy had style, the West German scooters were almost over-engineered, which led to more weight and more power than their Latin competitors.

## NSU

*Neckarsulm Stickmachen Union* (NSU) ranks alongside BMW and DKW as one of Germany's most famous motor cycle marques, with a reputation for high-quality products. During the first half of the 20th century, NSU often led the world with its design, innovation and production methods, to say nothing of its sporting successes, both before and after the Second World War.

The NSU story began in 1873, originally manufacturing mechanical knitting machines. By 1886 NSU were making bicycles; then in 1900, the first NSU motor cycle was produced using a Swiss ZL (Zedal) power unit. But soon NSU switched to engines of its own design, in both single and v-twin configuration.

In the first decade of the 20th century, a large proportion of NSU's production was exported – for example, British riders purchased almost a quarter of its production in 1906! During the 1914–18 war NSU turned its production over to munitions, but after the conflict soon returned to motor cycles. In 1929 the famous British designer Walter Moore joined NSU from Norton, only returning to Great Britain in 1939.

During the Second World War NSU built thousands of motor cycles and pedal cycles for the German armed forces, as well as aircraft components, but its strangest wartime creation was the *Kettenrad* (chain track) motor cycle.

Unlike many German rivals, NSU was able to restart production quickly after the war's end, helped by operating a repair centre for the American army!

## The NSU-Lambretta Licence Agreement

Like rivals Hoffman, who concluded an agreement to build Vespas under licence in West Germany from Piaggio, NSU struck a licence deal with Innocenti in Milan to manufacture the Lambretta, and initially these two companies dominated German scooter production.

Essentially, the model that appeared was identical to the Italian edition. For the German market, however, the metalwork was manufactured by Volkswagen. The power unit being supplied to begin with was direct from Innocenti, but later NSU proposed that it should manufacture the engine itself – which Innocenti agreed to.

In Italy, the model was referred to as the Type C, this having a 123cc (52x58mm) piston-ported, single-cylinder, two-stroke engine, giving 4.5bhp at 4,500rpm. Transmission was a twist-grip-controlled three-speed gearbox, with shaft final drive.

As Michael Dregni pointed out:

> The Germans had no patience for certain features of the Lambretta that they found lacking in good teutonic over-engineering. Soon, NSU models surpassed the Innocenti Lambretta in the quality of brakes, Bosch 6-volt horn, Magura seats, and higher output, 30 watt flywheel magneto at a time when the Lambretta LC had only 25 watts.

*The Prima D was NSU's first in-house scooter, making its public bow at the Brussels Show in January 1956.*

NSU also added features such as a glove box behind the leg shield topped by a small facia featuring the ignition switch, speedometer, choke and even the luxury of a clock!

At the Frankfurt Show in October 1953, NSU introduced a new electric start version of its Lambretta – using two six-volt batteries in series. Then at the end of 1954, a 150cc version with 6.2bhp and a top speed of 52mph (84km/h) made its bow.

In December 1955 the Lambretta licence agreement expired after a total of 117,045 NSU-Lambretta machines had been built.

### The *Prima* is Launched

For some time it had been known that NSU would build its own scooter. This was launched at the Brussels Show in January 1956. At first glance the new machine, the *Prima* (first), appeared so like the original Lambretta that it was unofficially whispered at Brussels that the machine exhibited was no more than a stop-gap and that the *real* NSU model would not be ready for several months. This was in fact partly true – the model at Brussels was the *Prima* D and was essentially NSU's take on the Lambretta LD. The definitive NSU scooter, the *Prima* V would not appear for several months.

The engine was NSU's version of the shaft-drive Lambretta 150 and still had three speeds. And the only really major difference between it and what had gone before was the use of pressed steel front forks rather than Innocenti's steel-tube components.

In addition the handlebars were now enclosed and an electric start was standard equipment. During 1956 a total of 37,062 *Prima* Ds went out to the agent and dealer networks. And although not fast, it proved a supremely reliable and luxurious machine, which provided its owners with years of trouble-free service.

### Other *Prima* Models

The *Prima* V (five star) was introduced midway through 1957. And although bearing a family resemblance to the original *Prima* D, which in turn descended from the even earlier NSU–Lambretta, its basic concept was very different as it had an entirely new frame and a larger-capacity 174cc engine – again of new design.

The great success that the *Prima* V was to enjoy saw a couple of spin-offs: the *Prima* IIIK (1958–59) and the *Prima* KL (1959–60). The first these, the IIIK, was essentially a simplified, cheaper version of the *Prima* V with a smaller-capacity 146cc engine (achieved by reducing the bore size to 57mm) and a lower top speed. It also had a less luxurious specification and the bodywork was revised. K stood for *mit Kick-starter* (with kick-starter), the electric starter having been removed. There was also a dearth

**Drive better -**

**Drive Prima**

**Machines with a World Famous Name -**

Prima V · Prima III + IIIK    Prima D

NSU

*A 1958 NSU Prima brochure covering the V, III, IIIK and D versions.*

NSU launched the *Prima* V, or as it is more commonly known, *Fünfstern* (five star) in the summer of 1957. The newcomer was intended as a luxury scooter, up-to-the-minute in both appearance and specification, and had taken NSU's engineering team many months to design and develop.

To provide the *Prima* V with a sufficiently lively performance to hold its own with other traffic when ridden two-up, a displacement of 174cc (62x57.5mm) was selected for the single-cylinder, piston-port two-stroke engine. The engine-gear-transmission assembly was pivot-mounted to the frame and, to provide a low centre of gravity, and on the machine's centre-line, the cylinder was disposed horizontally and transversely, just ahead of the rear wheel. The cylinder head and barrel were cooled in the usual way on NSU scooters, by means of a fan located on the rotor of the 12-volt starter-generator at the front of the crankcase. With a compression ratio of 6.35:1, NSU claimed 9.5bhp. The electric starter components were of Bosch origin.

The engine drove a four-speed gearbox through a single-plate car-type clutch of large diameter and all-indirect pattern, the gearbox; employed helical-cut pinions for the top gear pair to ensure quiet running. The cam plate of the gear-change mechanism operated the selector forks directly and control was by way of a rocking pedal, which protruded through the nearside (left) footboard. Immediately aft of the rear bearing of the gearbox output shaft was situated the pinion of the spiral-bevel final reduction to the rear wheel, an arrangement that minimized the overall length of the power unit. This meant that no chains were used in the transmission system.

Rear wheel movement was controlled by a long, multi-rate spring with a co-axial hydraulic damper. Meanwhile, front suspension was by a tubular pivoted fork featuring a separate pivot on both sides. A single, hydraulically damped spring unit was fitted between the nearside (left) arm of the fork and the stanchion member. The wheels were of pressed-steel, scalloped out at intervals, NSU said, to provide less resistance to crosswinds, and had 10in diameter rims fitted with 3.50 section tyres.

Despite having some resemblance to the *Prima* D, the Five Star was more bulky, with a totally new tail end and much larger air intake slots, which were flanked by chromium-plated trim-work. The headlamp blended into the top of the steering head area below the handlebars,

The NSU Prima V brochure proclaims: 'A completely new Scooter!'

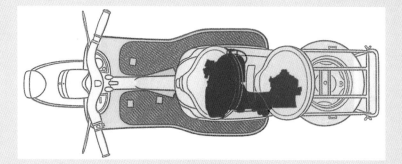

*The 175cc two-stroke engine was horizontally mounted and positioned exactly in the centre.*

whilst the comprehensive, sprung front mudguard turned with the wheel and on its top was mounted an oblong fog lamp – an unusual feature for a scooter.

Both cantilever-mounted the two separate saddles, provided a travel of almost 3in (75mm). Standard equipment included a rear-mounted spare wheel and carrier. The superbly designed handlebar layout echoed the *Prima* N, with its stub grips and concealed lever pivots. Below this, and on the rear of the weather shield, was a comprehensive instrument panel. This included the speedometer, ignition and lighting switch and the control for the carburettor starting device, together with a clock and warning lights for ignition and fuel level. The

**The new Prima - as you like it:**

Tastes, of course, differ and should not be agured about. That is why NSU offers the new Prima V in four different colours. These colours are not only just sprayed on; they are synthetic high-gloss finishes, applied in a scientifically controlled manner and treated by an infra-red process to retain their durable hard-gloss surface. This excellent finish is really wearresistant.

**Ride better — Ride NSU Prima V**

*The Prima V was offered in four colour schemes.*

fuel tank capacity was 2.6gal (12ltr).

Due to its greater weight and bulk, the Five Star was only marginally faster than the smaller-engined *Prima* N. *Motor Cycle* recorded a maximum speed of 56mph (90km/h) in a test published on 27 February 1958. The test considered, 'Electric starting, brisk performance, excellent handling and lavish equipment' as the machine's foremost attributes. Other notable features of the Five Star included unusually powerful brakes for a scooter. *Motor Cycle* also pointed out:

> Sensibly the *Prima* has no centre stand but is equipped with an excellent prop stand which would support the scooter safely under practically any conditions. For wheel-changing purposes there is a transversely pivoted jack so positioned that either wheel can be propped clear of the ground ... In short, the Five Star *Prima* is a magnificently equipped, luxury scooter equally well suited to suburban pottering and long-distance touring.

According to Michael Dregni, 'five star was recognized worldwide as the highest rating; the *Prima Fünfstern* was NSU's two-wheeled answer to Mercedes Benz. This was the scooter that the good German plutocrat could love, a blend of world-class engineering, luxury features and power.'

The British price in February 1958 was £249 19s. It was also imported in the USA by Butler & Smith of New York.

| Specification | 1958 NSU Prima V |
| --- | --- |
| Engine | Fan-cooled, two-stroke, single |
| Displacement | 174cc |
| Bore & stroke | 62x57.5mm |
| Gearbox | Four-speed, foot-change |
| Wheel size | 10in |
| Power | 9.5bhp |
| Maximum speed | 56mph (90km/h) |

*An April 1958 advertisement by the British NSU importers illustrating factory accessories for the Prima models.*

of brightwork, a black saddle and only one colour choice (ivory). In 1959 a *Lux* version, the KL, was offered, this featuring an electric start, chrome trim, a two-tone colour scheme and an optional dual seat assembly.

### End of The Road

During 1960 the NSU engineering team had begun work on a new top-of-the-range scooter called the Maxima, the name reflecting the joining together of the words Maxi and *Prima*.

The new design was powered by the latest version of the 175cc *Prima* V engine, which by now was producing 10.5bhp.

However, NSU was rapidly switching production to cars, and so it took the decision to stop selling scooters, which meant that the Maxima project remained a prototype only.

In conclusion, discounting the licence-built

*Maicomobil*

*The 'Auto on Two Wheels' was Maico's claim for its Mobil, and one can see why from this period drawing.*

NSU-Lambrettas, NSU built a total of 160,631 *Prima* models.

## Maico

Two young brothers, Otto and Wilhelm Maisch, saw an opportunity to begin building bicycles in their small workshop during the height of the Great Depression in 1931. By the mid-1930s they had added motor cycles. This was so successful that at the beginning of the 1940s they had a new factory at Pfaffingen. However, with BMW, DKW, NSU and Zündapp already building motor cycles for the army, Maico was enlisted into manufacturing aircraft components for the Luftwaffe.

After the end of the conflict, Maico returned to motor cycles, the first of which was built in 1947.

### The Maico-Mobil

However, it was not until the Reulingen Show in June 1950 that Maico introduced the proto-type of what it called an 'auto on two wheels'. The Maico-Mobil scooter was unique and, when production began the following year, there was nothing else like it on the road. Their claim was no idle boast, as it combined maximum weather protection and carrying capacity for both the rider and passenger that was superior to any other two-wheeler of the time.

This is how the company described the machine:

The Maico-Mobil was created as a wholly new type of motor vehicle in which the amenities of the automobile are combined with the mobility and modest requirements of the motor cycle. The Maico-Mobil is not a scooter but a motor cycle with a body giving a high degree of protection against the weather. It is no strain on the rider to travel 300 miles a day on the 14in tyre vehicle. He does not get his shoes or trousers splashed or muddy and likewise, his hands and gloves are protected against wet and cold. Such a mode of transportation enables the businessman to retain his neat appearance in all weather and over long distances, on poor roads.

The first production Maico-Mobil of 1951 was powered by a 148cc (57x58mm) fan-cooled, single-cylinder two-stroke engine, producing 6.5bhp at 4,800rpm. The gearbox was a three-speeder. However, with its bulk and weight – 253lb (115kg) – this was soon found to be inadequate.

### Larger Engines

At the end of 1954, the 150 was axed in favour of two new engines of 173cc (61x59.5mm) and 197cc (65x59.5mm), giving 8.5bhp and 10.9bhp respectively. At the same time the gearbox was changed to four speeds.

But otherwise, the Maico-Mobil remained largely as before, which meant primary and final drives by chain, a steel-tubular frame, 14in wheels, telescopic front forks and a rear

## The Maico-Mobil

The first ever photograph of the revolutionary Maico-Mobil appeared in the German magazine, *Das Auto* in late spring 1950. It had a 148cc (57x58mm) two-stroke engine (without fan-cooling) and twin-port cylinder barrel, 6.5bhp and a speed of 53mph (85km/h).

Launched as a prototype at the Reulingen show in June 1950, the Maico-Mobil was one of the stranger devices created by the post-war German two-wheel industry. It featured truly cavernous bodywork accommodating the engine assembly, a spare wheel and enough room for a considerable amount of luggage. At the front was an equally massive built-in fairing and screen. Although now recognized as a scooter, in the early days Maico went to some lengths to tell prospective buyers that beneath its bodywork, the Maico-Mobil was really a fully enclosed motor cycle, with a full duplex frame and telescopic fork.

As an example, one of the early sales brochures said, 'not a scooter but a motor cycle with a body giving a high degree of protection against the weather'. The company saw the Mobil as 'The auto on two wheels' and claimed it was quite possible to travel 300 miles (500km), a day without any strain on the rider.

The potential of 300 miles in one day falls into perspective when it is realized that the original prototype was powered by a conventional air-cooled 148cc two-stroke single. This was essentially one of the twin-port engines used on the M150 motor cycle, but with a three-speed, hand-change gearbox. The engine was mounted so that it almost sat on the swinging arm, which pivoted on a pair of coil springs mounted in a similar position to the monoshock unit found on one of the latest motor cycles of today.

However, power from the engine was simply not enough for what, after all, was intended as a serious touring machine, but by the time the Maico-Mobil entered production in 1951, it had addressed this problem. Again a single-cylinder two-stroke, but now fan-cooled, and with new bore and stroke dimensions of 61x59.5mm, giving a displacement of 174cc. With a single-port iron cylinder and alloy head it developed a more respectable 9bhp at 5,300rpm.

Air for the forced-draught cooling was drawn around the cowled cylinder by a multi-bladed cast-alloy fan. This was driven by a rubber belt from a pulley on an extension of the nearside (left) end of the crankshaft. In the unit with the engine was a three-speed hand-operated gearbox, whilst the rear drive was by chain – not oil-bath, but only partially enclosed by a mild steel cover.

Car-type interchangeable 14in cast-alloy wheels employed 3.00 section tyres, which were bolted into aluminium brake hubs. A notable standard fitment was indicators mounted on the outer section of the front fairing panels. Both fairing and trafficators were of aluminium construction.

The Maico-Mobil was given a power boost for 1954, with an increase in engine size to 197cc (65x59.5mm) and perhaps even more importantly, a four-speed, foot-change gearbox. At

*A Maico-Mobil photograph, circa 1954, of a street scene in Germany.*

*Maico-Mobil and Mascot on the Maico Owners Club stand at the International Classic Motor Cycle Show, Stafford, April 2006.*

the same time, a switch was made from alloy to steel pressings for the wheels, inner dash and wrap-over centre section, whilst the tyres now had a wider 3.25 section.

*Motor Cycling* tested a 200 Maico-Mobil in its 22 November 1956 issue, recording a maximum speed of 60mph (96.5km/h). They also found, 'The steering of the Maico Mobil is almost automatic and it can be heeled over with perfect confidence. The shielding offers considerable protection for the rider.'

Once one got over the unusual nature of the Maico-Mobil it was a surprisingly effective machine. I found that weather protection for both rider (and passenger) was superb and that I had mistakenly considered the machine to be cumbersome and awkward to handle. The positioning of the fuel tank over the front wheel

provided positive steering, whilst features such control cables that are adjustable by hand at the handlebar ends are typical of the detail to be found. All in all, the Maico-Mobil is probably the least understood and underestimated scooter of all – until one rides it.

The British price, including purchase tax was then £198.8s.

| Specification | 1957 Maico Mobil |
|---|---|
| Engine | Fan-cooled, two-stroke, single |
| Displacement | 197cc |
| Bore & stroke | 65x59.5mm |
| Gearbox | Four-speed, foot-change |
| Wheel size | 14in |
| Power | 10.3bhp |
| Maximum speed | 60mph (96.5km/h) |

*What was underneath all that bodywork.*

Billed as 'The most powerful German motor scooter', the Maicoletta was officially announced in January 1955 and, together with the equally new Maico Blizzard motor cycle, made full use of the technical development that had gone into it, winning the 250cc German Motocross Championship title.

Its public début came at The Brussels Show and in a report published in *Motor Cycle* dated 20 January 1955, it was mentioned that its 247cc fan-cooled engine was similar to one of the Maico motor cycles. In fact, what it really meant was that the new scooter used a detuned version of the motocross unit.

Both the Blizzard and Maicoletta (in 250cc guise) shared a very similar engine specification (except for fan-cooling) of 248cc (67x70mm). But whilst the motor cycle followed earlier Maico practices, the new Maicoletta certainly did not. It combined the comfort and weather protection of the scooter with the performance of a motor cycle. And because of these attributes it soon won a strong and loyal following. In 1955, a 174cc (61x59.5mm) version was added.

The first British test of a Maicoletta appeared shortly afterwards by *Motor Cycling*. Tester John Griffiths was truly impressed. On every single point, save operation of the centre stand, the test scooter was praised lavishly. Eye appeal, quality, handling, performance, and braking were all of the highest standard. And certainly, this was one scooter that really seemed to have benefited positively from its motor cycle parentage.

John Griffiths highlighted just what an impact the machine had caused whilst in his care:

> Riding the Maicoletta was almost an embarrassment. On numerous occasions motorcyclists – particularly those of the enthusiastic clubman type – surprised by its turn of speed, came up alongside for a second look. And at a standstill it proved a magnet to all kinds of people, attracted by its unusually good looks and pleasing finish of light blue and grey, with red trimming.

Although never used on a production Maico motor cycle, a 277cc capacity engine was available on the Maicoletta scooter from autumn 1957 (mainly due to the request of the British importers). This size was achieved by a 4mm increase in cylinder bore size, giving dimensions of 71x70mm, and was the only difference from the unit that powered the smaller 175 and 250cc models. All three Maicolettas had long-skirt pistons. They were also all fitted with electric starters, rather than the kick-starters found on Maico motor cycles.

Other details of the Maicoletta's specification included: chain primary and final drives; Bing

## MAICOLETTA

The most powerful German Motor Scooter

175 + 250 cc.

*A 1956 model year brochure proclaims: 'Maicoletta – The Most Powerful German Motor Scooter'. This was no idle boost, as the 250cc version could top 68mph (109km/h).*

*A Maicoletta factory photograph that illustrates the imposing size of the machine.*

carburettors; tubular steel frames with a large diameter main tube; pressed-steel panelling; split 14in rims with 3.50 section tyres; petroil lubrication; 6-volt electrics; telescopic front forks controlled by coil springs; rear springing (by swinging fork, movement controlled by coil springs) with hydraulic damping; and a 2.6gal (11.5ltr) fuel tank located under the large dual seat and aft of the engine. Maico sources claimed a power-output for the 250 version of 14bhp at 5,000rpm and a maximum speed of 68mph (109km/h).

British imports began in August 1956, by Maico Distributors (GB) of London. The Maicoletta was also imported into the USA with some success, by Whizzer International of Michigan.

The Maicoletta remained in production until 1966.

| Specification | 1958 Maicoletta 250 |
|---|---|
| Engine | Fan-cooled, two-stroke, single |
| Displacement | 247cc |
| Bore & stroke | 67x70mm |
| Gearbox | Four-speed, foot-change |
| Wheel size | 14in |
| Power | 14bhp |
| Maximum speed | 70mph (113km/h) |

swinging fork (with twin shocks), and 6–volt electrics.

According to Michael Dregni, 'The Mobil provided motor cycle handling and scooter performance and weather protection with styling like the Hindenburg Zeppelin on wheels!'

Interestingly, one Maico-Mobil owner was King Hussain of Jordon, himself a keen two-wheel enthusiast.

## The Maicoletta

However, the real Maico scooter classic was the famous Maicoletta, which was launched at the 1955 Brussels Show. It was and still is, consid-

ered by many to have been the ultimate performance scooter ever to reach series production. It was built in 175, 250 and 277cc engine sizes (one of the largest engines ever to find its way into a scooter chassis during the classic era), the latter specifically for the British market. Performance-wise both the 250 and 277cc versions could top a genuine 70mph (113km/h).

The Maicoletta was one of the longest-lived single scooter model types, having an eleven-year production life – thanks to examples being built in Great Britain after production had ceased in West Germany.

As British scooter expert Mike Webster

*The Heinkel Tourist was notable for its combination of a four-stroke engine and a supremely comfortable ride. It first went on sale in 149cc form in 1953, followed by the definitive 173cc version in 1954.*

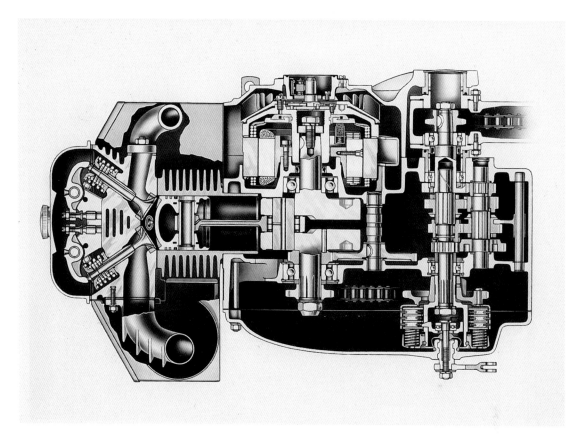

*An engineering overview of the overhead-valve Heinkel Tourist engine and transmission.*

remarked, 'At 14kg [31lb] the Maicoletta is no lightweight. It has hydraulic telescopic forks and rear swinging-arm suspension. In every way the Maicoletta is a long way from the rationale of the lightweight Italians. It is a machine designed for long-distance, high-speed travel and in this respect, it delivers.'

It was a scooter that was loved by scooter and motor cycle fans alike, and many were sold on the recommendations of other owners. Truly, the Maicoletta was something very special.

## Glas

Glas was a major producer of scooters and small four-wheeled German cars, whose scooter could trace its origins back to 1951. Marketed under the Goggo label, all were of high quality, the scooters using 123, 148 and 197cc Ilo single-cylinder two-stroke engines. Between 1951 and 1956 a total of 46,181 models was produced. There were also various versions of the *Lastenroller* (goods scooter), which was essentially a scooter front section with a truck rear half.

However, it was the twin-cylinder 247, 296 and 395cc *Goggomobil* light cars that really

# The Heinkel Tourist

As a four-stroke – and a good one – the Heinkel Tourist has always been viewed as a scooter for the connoisseur.

Initial development had commenced in 1952 and the first version, the 150 101AO, to be marketed as the Tourist, was first announced in early 1953; however, first deliveries did not arrive on the German home market until January 1954.

*The Tourist in 149cc form was first announced in early 1953, but deliveries did not begin until January 1954. That August the engine was increased in size to 174cc. Production finally ended in late 1965.*

A machine that more than lived up to Germany's high standards of engineering, the Tourist was neatly styled, its design and construction owing much to Heinkel's aviation background. Its frame was of tubular-steel construction enclosed by sheet-metal pressings. Front suspension was by telescopic forks and the rear by a single hydraulically controlled unit operated by a pivoted fork. The 8in wheels were of the split-rim type with 4.00 section tyres. The rear panelling was quickly detachable (with only two bolts) and provided access to a partitioned luggage compartment and the fan-cooled 149cc (59x54.5mm) overhead-valve single-cylinder engine. Producing 7.2bhp at 5,200rpm, it provided a maximum speed of 56mph (90km/h). A three-speed gearbox was built in unit with the engine and operated via a handlebar twist-grip mechanism. Both primary and final drives were by chain, the latter containing an aluminium casting incorporating an oil bath.

The ignition was by coil/battery (6-volt) with automatic advance and retard. Hinged on a locking platform, the dual seat could be raised to provide access to the fuel filler cap.

In June 1954 the Tourist was converted from 6 to 12 volts with an electric start – the original 6-volt system only had a kick-starter.

However, the 101AO was superseded just two months later by the model 102 A1. This brought an increase in displacement to 174cc (60x61.5mm) and, coupled with the replacement of the original Pallas 18/10 carburettor to a Bing 1/18/5 instrument, saw the power rise to 9.2bhp at 5,500rpm. However, the 102 A1 continued to feature only three speeds, all the other changes being purely cosmetic.

The first official imports into Great Britain began at the end of October 1955, when the famous British motor cycle manufacturer Excelsior began bringing in supplies marketed as Excelsior-Heinkel, priced at £239 8s. By the time the Tourist was marketed in Great Britain, the specification had again been uprated, with four speeds and a return to a Pallas carburettor, whilst the wheel diameter had been increased to 10in. These changes provided improvements to both overall performance and road holding abilities.

When *Motor Cycle News* tested a Tourist in its 8 August 1956 issue, the British price had increased to £247 7s 7d or, with clock and spare

Le HEINKEL-TOURIST est non seulement le seul scooter à 4 temps, mais aussi le scooter le plus vendu en Allemagne. A l'origine de son succès se trouve une heureuse synthèse de puissance, d'exceptionnelle économie et de perfection des lignes.

## DONNEES TECHNIQUES

**Moteur**

| | |
|---|---|
| Type | 4 temps |
| Nombre de cylindres | 1 |
| Alésage | 60,0 mm |
| Course | 61,5 mm |
| Cylindrée | 174 cm³ |
| Puissance | 9,2 CV. à 5500 t/min. |
| Refroidissement | Par soufflerie |
| Allumage | Batterie-démarreur-dynamo avec avance automatique 12 volts, 90 watts |
| Carburateur | à aiguille, avec pompe d'accélération |
| Réservoir d'essence | 11,5 litres dont 2 l. de réserve |

**Boîte de vitesses**

Commande par poignée tournante au guidon, 4 vitesses.
Rapports totaux de démultiplication:
1e. vit. 18,05:1
2e. vit. 10,60:1
3e. vit. 7,10:1
4e. vit. 5,13:1

**Partie cycle**

Cadre en tubes d'acier entretoisé
Suspension avant fourche télescopique avec amortisseur hydraulique
Suspension arrière bras oscillant fermé jambage à ressort avec amortisseur télescopique hydraulique
Roues 2 + roue de secours
Pneus 4,00 x 10"
Freins à tambour, mâchoires intérieures

**Dimensions et poids**

| | |
|---|---|
| Longueur | 2200 mm |
| Hauteur | 1150 mm |
| Largeur | 840 mm |
| Poids à vide | 156 kg |
| Poids total admissible (solo) | 350 kg |

**Puissance et consommation**

Pouvoir en côte en 1e. vitesse env. 32%
Consommation d'essence à 70 km/h. 3,0 l./100 km.

Consommation du carburant

Accélération

*A Belgian market brochure showing technical features of the 175 Tourist. The four-stroke engine and 12-volt electrics, amongst other attributes, made it a firm favourite with scooter enthusiasts.*

wheel (both popular accessories), £260 7s 7d. *Motor Cycle News* was impressed, saying:

A great deal of attention has obviously been given to detail features of the design. Fitted to the front cowl, just above the headlamp, is a hinged luggage grid which can be used to carry, say, a small holdall and which hinges flush against the cowl when not in use, while under the seat is a compartment large enough to hold, in addition to the tool kit, such items as gloves, a scarf and goggles … Throughout the whole machine the finish and quality of workmanship are of a very high order indeed and

although the price is rather high, it must be borne in mind that the standard specification – including, as it does a self starter – is extremely luxurious.

By the 1959 season the control cables on the handlebars were fully enclosed, covered by a streamlined moulding. 1960 saw the final changes to the specification of the Tourist, referred to as the Mark II or 103A2. Mechanically, the only changes were an improved, larger-capacity air filter, increased fuel tank capacity, and direction indicators. Styling was drastically changed, the rear panelling now featuring squarer lines with an entirely new rear light cluster, superior padding for the dual seat, a slightly altered headlamp and a much revised trim.

First imports into Great Britain of this model did not begin until February 1962, by new concessionaires Hans Motors of London.

The Tourist was widely used in scooter sport. Heinkels competed in 108 international and national events between 1958 and 1960 – often against fierce competition from motor cycles. In this time they achieved a staggering 349 gold medals, 67 gold team awards, 101 silver medals and 62 bronze medals. Indeed, a Tourist ridden by Don Noys finished first in its class and second overall in Great Britain's first ever scooter race, held at Crystal Palace, London, in 1960.

Production ceased in late 1965, but Hans Motors were still selling machines in Great Britain as late as 1967. As for Heinkel, they had by now returned to the aviation sector.

| Specification | 1965 Heinkel Tourist A2 |
|---|---|
| Engine | Fan-cooled, overhead-valve, single |
| Displacement | 174cc |
| Bore & stroke | 60x61.5mm |
| Gearbox | Four-speed, foot-change |
| Wheel size | 10in |
| Power | 9.5bhp |
| Maximum speed | 60mph (96.5km/h) |

*Heinkel also offered smaller, two-stroke-engined scooters. The first of these, which was produced in 1957, was the 112 with a capacity of 125cc.*

made the name of the company. Over a twelve-year period from 1955–67 a total of 357,200 were sold.

Then founder Hans Glas sold, at the height of his success, to BMW in 1966; following this, all the Dingolfing plant's machine tools and production facilities were shipped to South Africa to establish a BMW facility in that country.

## Heinkel

Ernst Heinkel had started his company in 1922 and went on to design many of the Fatherland's most famous aircraft, including the He 111 bomber.

Together with Messerschmitt, another major German aircraft manufacturer, Heinkel was banned from building aircraft in the immediate aftermath of the Second World War, and so both turned their hands to personal transport – motor cycles, micro-cars or

scooters. Messerschmitt built their famous *Kabenroller* (cabin scooter) micro-car and, from the mid-1950s, the Italian Vespa scooter when Hoffman didn't renew its licence agreement with Piaggio.

## Entering The Scooter World

In common with manufacturers in Italy and Japan, Heinkel chose to manufacture scooters when the war ended. However, unlike Piaggio and its Vespa for example, Heinkel made a slow start, with development beginning only in 1951. The Tourist scooter with a 149cc four-stroke engine was launched in January 1953, followed in 1954 by the 49cc Perla moped (the latter of technical interest because it had an aluminium frame). The Tourist later became available with a 174cc engine.

During 1956, Heinkel launched their *Kabine* micro-car, with car-type steering and independent suspension, powered by the 174cc Tourist engine, or a 198cc version of the

*Dürkopp were a long-established engineering firm that also built motorcycles and scooters. Named the Diana, Dürkopp's scooter arrived in 1954. These wonderful factory colour prints taken in 1955 illustrate the period beautifully.*

same unit. Like the BMW Isetta, access was via a single front-opening door.

Over 100,000 Tourists were built and were so reliable that the company offered plaques for mileages achieved: gold for 100,000km (62,140 miles) and silver for 75,000km (46,605 miles), but the bronze

for 50,000km (31,070 miles) was soon discontinued because it became apparent that it was easily within every owner's grasp – the scooter was proving bullet-proof. Its excellent service record also meant that the Tourist attracted widespread use by the German police service.

*The Diana was a high-quality product, with many interesting and practical features. This is a 1960 Diana Sport.*

Of all the German scooters manufactured during the classic period, the Dürkopp Diana is probably the most stylish. Somehow it managed to combine German engineering abilities with Italian styling flair. And it also had an excellent turn of speed which, combined with superb handling, made it one of the very best of all small-wheeled models.

The Diana first went on sale in 1954. and when Mick Woollett tested an example for *Motor Cycle News* in the 10 October 1956 issue, he had this to say:

The scooter has certainly come a long way since the first continental models appeared on our roads some seven or eight years ago. This was brought home by me by the road test I have just carried out with a Dürkopp Diana, a new [to Great Britain] scooter which not only has a motor cycle performance, but has eliminated the two main faults of its predecessors – poor steering and gear change … The four-speed

gearbox is a joy to use. The ratios are perfectly suited to the engine and the foot control is really positive. Never once did it slip out of gear or miss a 'cog' when changing. The foot control is situated on the left footboard and sticks straight up. You push forward to change down and back to change up.

An interesting feature of the transmission was the patented neutral selector. This selected neutral from any gear and the mechanism was so designed that it also found neutral between first and second, so that restarting presented no difficulties.

Although the Diana's clutch operation was on the heavy side, engagement for moving off was positive, smooth and without snatch.

The single-cylinder, fan-cooled engine with a chrome-plated alloy barrel displaced 194cc (64x61mm). The first version put out 9.5bhp at 5,500rpm – the Sport variant later giving an additional 2.5bhp at the same engine revolutions. Dürkopp sources said the additional power had been obtained by skimming the cylinder head in order to increase the compres-

*The neatly contoured front mudguard was both stylish and effective.*

sion ratio, opening out the ports and advancing the ignition timing.

In common with the vast majority of German scooters, the Diana was well silenced, the exhaust gases travelling through a section of the frame before entering the twin silencers that occupied the space beneath the two foot-boards. The unit was rubber-mounted and no vibration could normally be felt. Final drive to the rear wheel was by a totally enclosed chain.

The Diana was provided with a 12-volt Noris electric starter, the batteries of which were stowed under the pillion seat. A kick-start was also available for emergencies and, when not in use, the pedal folded inwards to double up as the previously mentioned neutral selector.

There was a special Bing carburettor, which incorporated an automatic starting device, whilst the engine was accessible by the removal of two quick-release side panels, no tools being needed for this task.

As Mick Woollett went on to describe in the *Motor Cycle News* test, 'Steering was inclined to be on the heavy side at low speed, but at medium and high speeds it was the equal of most motor cycles and superior to some ... The machine could be heeled into bumpy bands with complete confidence and this, combined with the slick gear change, made open road and country lane a real joy.'

The wheels were 10in and shod with 3.50 section tyres. Springing was by trailing arm at the front and swinging arm at the rear (both hydraulically damped).

As for performance, the standard Diana could reach 57mph (92km/h), whilst the Sport version could achieve 65mph (105km/h).

When *Motor Cycling* tested a Diana Sport in its 23 April 1959 issue, its headline read: 'Performance as Bright as its Colour!', this being due to the scarlet red finish and a sporting performance. Even though the tester was not impressed by the 'slow-action twist-grip ... two "grabs" being necessary to wind it from closed to fully open', virtually every other aspect of the Diana Sport impressed, in particular the comfort and lightness of the steering – the latter being described as being, 'likened to flying a Tiger Moth – does everything you ask, and doesn't try to impose any ideas of its own'. The report ended, 'Dürkopp have set out to produce a scooter for the sporting rider and they have attained their objective in a highly satisfying manner.'

Production of the standard version ceased in 1959, the same year as the 171cc Diana TS made its bow. The Sport and TS models were last manufactured in late 1960, but customers were able to buy the Sport as late as 1962 in Great Britain, where imports were handled from 1956 onwards by Diana Concessionaires of Surrey.

| Specification | 1960 Dürkopp Diana Sport |
|---|---|
| Engine | Fan-cooled, two-stroke, single |
| Displacement | 194cc |
| Bore & stroke | 64x61mm |
| Gearbox | Four-speed, foot-change |
| Wheel size | 10in |
| Power | 12bhp |
| Maximum speed | 65mph (104.5km/h) |

The Sport model can be easily identified by this carburettor intake, fitted  to maximize performance.

A Diana brochure produced in April 1956.

# The Zündapp Bella

The Zündapp Bella was one of the toughest and most reliable scooters ever made, débuting in May 1953. Designated the Bella *Motor Roller* (motor scooter), it was to prove a major success story for the company, with the basic design continuing until 1964, by which time a total of 130,680 had been manufactured during its eleven-year life span.

The first model was the Bella 150, or R150 with a displacement of 147cc (57x58mm), a 0.8in (20mm) Bing carburettor and a maximum speed of 50mph (80km/h). Its piston-port two-stroke engine featured a three-ring piston, cast-iron cylinder and alloy head.

The Bella featured geared primary drive to a four-speed gearbox in unit with the engine and controlled by a foot-operated rocking pedal, whilst the final drive chain was fully enclosed in a case arranged to pivot with the swinging arm fork rear suspension assembly.

Open coil suspension springs were employed, controlled by a single hydraulic damper fitted on the nearside of the rear fork. The front wheel was mounted in leading-axle telescopic front forks, and the relatively large 12in alloy wheels with 6in drum brakes front and rear.

The frame took an unusual form, principally consisting of a large diameter downtube and two backbone members arching over the engine and rear wheel. Over this frame was

*The Bella was equally suited to commuting to work and to undertaking serious touring holidays.*

fitted pressed-steel bodywork offering a large expanse of protection both front and rear. Included in the body was a fuel tank with a capacity of 2gal (9ltr).

The Bella's engine unit was based on Zündapp's motor cycle and did not have fan-cooling. Instead the cooling air passed around the front mudguard, through a tunnel to the engine. The air then exited via grills to the rear of the seat and slots in the side panels. This particular design feature had been 'borrowed' from the Italian Parilla scooter.

The Bella was extremely well-engineered and the early models in particular made wide use of aluminium castings not only for the trim but also for the footboards. As the well-known British scooter historian Mike Webster said, 'The motor is virtually unburstable and, given minimal maintenance will seemingly run for ever.'

Cast aluminium grilles on each side of the rear wheel were hinged so they would fold down to become pannier luggage supports, and a spare

*The Bella was another example of German engineering at its best.*

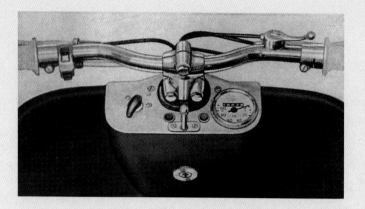

*The practical Bella dashboard with speedometer and switches.*

wheel and carrier could be purchased at additional cost.

By May 1954 no fewer than 10,000 Bellas had been sold and this spurred Zündapp into increasing the appeal by creating new versions, including a 200cc machine incorporating numerous changes and dubbed the R200. To achieve the larger capacity, bore and stroke had been increased to 64x62mm respectively, which gave slightly over-square dimensions. The crankshaft assembly had been strengthened to withstand the greater power output of 10bhp at 5,200rpm. The transmission (primary drive and clutch) was also strengthened.

An important modification, which now also featured on the 150 Bella, was the adoption of a 90-watt flywheel generator in place of the original 60-watt component.

By early 1954 a stripped Bella, the Suburbanetta, was on sale in the USA.

For the 1956 season there was the introduction of revised bodywork, a new frame, dual seats and an electric start 12-volt system, whilst the model numbers changed from 150/200 to 151/201. But the really big news was that both the 151 and 201 gained a pivoted (single-sided suspension unit) front fork. However, to confuse the issue, the export version continued with the telescopic forks for some time thereafter.

The 200 Bella was recoded the 203 and the 151 became the 153 for the 1957 season, and then a year later the 203 became the 204, with the 153 becoming the 154. On the 204 model, although the capacity, plus bore and stroke measurements remained unchanged, there was a new crankcase and the cylinder was inclined from the vertical by thirty degrees.

At the end of 1961, the R175S was introduced with a new 174cc (60x62mm) engine size, which produced 11bhp at 5,400rpm. Likewise, the 204 became the 200 551–026 and later the 560–025. These were the fastest Bellas manufactured, producing 13.4bhp. But both these and the new 175 sold in only small numbers, as by the beginning of the 1960s scooter sales all around Europe were falling rapidly. The last Bella model was built in 1964.

*Cutaway drawing showing technical features of the Bella.*

| Specification | 1961 Zündapp Bella 204 |
| --- | --- |
| Engine | Air-cooled, two-stroke, single |
| Displacement | 198cc |
| Bore & stroke | 64x62mm |
| Gearbox | Four-speed, foot-change |
| Wheel size | 12in |
| Power | 12bhp |
| Maximum speed | 58mph (93km/h) |

*Zündapp's Bella series (a 1956 R151 is shown) was produced from 1953 until the mid-1960s, with 147, 174 and 198cc engine sizes.*

### The 112 and 150

Although the Tourist remained in production, Heinkel decided to also offer smaller-capacity scooters. The first, the 112 (but actually a 125) arrived in 1957, but was to prove an expensive failure. It, like the 150, which made its début in 1960, was to use four-stroke power like its older Tourist brothers.

Actually, in retrospect, the 112 had far superior lines to the 150, the latter trying to be a cross between the lightweight Italian scooters and over-modern styling of the rear end. As Michael Dregni commented when comparing it with the 112, 'The 150, on the other hand,

took a stab at new innovative scooter lines and failed miserably. The engine put out a decent 9hp for a maximum speed of 85km/h, but the lines and excessive two-tone make for a gaudy, at best, exterior.'

In January 1958, Ernst Heinkel died aged 70, but scooter and micro-car production continued. Both the 150 and Tourist models lived on until 1965.

### Dürkopp

The Dürkopp marque was one of the true pioneers of German motorcycling. Founded in Bielefeld in 1867 by Nikolaus Dürkopp, the company made bicycles from 1889 and motor cycles as early as 1901. By 1905 Dürkopp not only offered singles and v-twins, but an inline four-cylinder model.

Unlike many other rivals who also built motor cycles, Dürkopp was a flourishing general engineering concern and not wholly reliant upon its two-wheeled business.

Dürkopp ceased motor cycle production just prior to the outbreak of the Great War in 1914, but resumed during the 1930s with bicycles powered by auxiliary 'clip-on' engines of 60, 75 and 98cc displacements. Pukka motor cycles were not offered again until 1949 when models powered by 98cc Sachs, 125cc Ardie and Ilo engines appeared.

In 1951 Dürkopp introduced a brand-new 150cc motor cycle powered by an in-house power unit, quickly followed by similar 175 and 200cc versions. From then on no further proprietary engines were used.

### The Diana

The Diana scooter arrived in 1954, with a mass of publicity. And like the Heinkel Tourist, Maico Maicoletta, and Zündapp Bella it was destined to become one of the great German scooters of its day.

The model was an exceptionally high-quality product, offering a stylish and fast

*Zündapp even sold a Bella and sidecar combination as a complete package.*

performance which, combined with excellent handling qualities, made the Diana the equal to any scooter on the road.

The Diana was also the cornerstone of Dürkopp's two-wheeled business during the mid-1950s boom and helped it to weather the depression that followed, when most of the firm's other models were taken out of production.

Production of the various Diana models ceased in 1960, by which time 24,963 machines had been manufactured.

## Zündapp

Founded in September 1917, *Zünderland Apparatebau*, or as it was better known,

Zündapp, began as a joint venture between three established firms at the height of the First World War, to manufacture fuzes for artillery guns.

At the conflict's end, Zündapp struggled to find a commercial product. It was acquired by Fritz Neumeyer in 1919 and the task of finding a new product line was solved in 1921, when it built its first motor cycle, the forerunner of some three million other powered two-wheelers over the next sixty-three years.

By the late 1930s Zündapp was rivalling the mighty BMW marque for popularity – and often exceeding the latter in terms of actual production figures.

In 1951, Zündapp became interested in joining the ranks of the scooter manufacturers and developed a prototype example, but this never reached production status. After this the company studied scooter trends in Italy rather than its homeland, the result being based on a Parilla design as Zündapp considered that both Lambretta and Vespa had been copied enough already.

In terms of model types and production numbers, Zündapp was the second largest manufacturer of German scooters during the period covered by this book. Its production was dominated by the superb Bella, which was built over many years in a variety of model designations and engine sizes.

*Der Roller für den Motorradfahrer* (the scooter for the motorcyclist) – unlike many other manufacturers', this claim was fully justified, with the Bella combining the good points of the two types of machines perfectly. Whilst it had all the practical advantages of the scooter, Bella owners also benefited from excellent handling and, at least in the larger 200 engine size, enough power to transport two in comfort.

**Production Begins**

The first model to enter production was the Bella in 147cc form, which was launched in spring of 1953. But what really set Zündapp scooter sales on their way was the big hit made by the new 201 version when it took the International Frankfurt Show by storm in October 1953. Typical press reports of the period recorded that in the 200cc field the show's thunder had been stolen by Zündapp and that a test run proved that the Bella handled as well as any motor cycle, indeed better than most. It was also noted that acceleration was surprisingly brisk and the brakes were smooth and progressive.

**Other Designs**

Owing to the huge success achieved by its Bella, Zündapp designed and built a new 125cc scooter in 1955 using a horizontal engine.

Although a great deal of the research and development budget was taken up by this project, it was ultimately discontinued. Instead, the company continued work on making the Bella even better.

It was not until 1964 that the company launched two new machines to take the place of the Bella, which was to be discontinued. The new scooters were based on the Lambretta Slimline series with quickly detachable side panels, the headlamp on the handlebars, and smaller 10in wheels (the Bella employed 12in components) and handlebar gear change.

A major departure from the Italian design was the use of a much smaller engine size – 50cc. The engine was based on the existing Zündapp Falconette moped unit. Known as the Roller 50, it had three speeds and produced 2.9bhp at 4,900rpm, whilst the more expensive four-speed RS50 Super put out 4.6bhp at 7,000rpm. But in truth the later models were mere shadows in both size and ability of the much-loved Bella series. However, development of both 50s ran through until the mid-1980s when Zündapp came into financial difficulties and the German factory's plant and machinery were sold to the Chinese.

**Adler**

Based in Frankfurt, Adler was established by Heinrich Kleyer in 1886 to manufacture bicycles. The fledgling company began to supplement this business with typewriter production from 1895. Five years later, Adler joined the ranks of the automobile pioneers and manufactured its first car; then in 1902, it tried its hand at motor cycles.

The first powered two-wheeler used imported French De Dion engines, but Adler soon developed its own single and v-twin power units.

However, its motor cycles did not achieve high enough levels of sales and from the end

*The Victoria Peggy used a 198cc single-cylinder, two-stroke engine that it shared with the company's Swing motorcycle. An unusual feature of both was the push-button gear change mechanism.*

of 1907 until the late 1940s, Adler concentrated upon pedal cycles, cars and typewriters.

Adler's new motor cycle, the M100 (98cc) made its début in 1950. This was followed by a stream of new machines, culminating with the innovative and exciting M250 in 1952. This, it is generally agreed, was the first modern parallel twin design of the post-war era and was later to inspire several manufacturers including Yamaha in Japan and Ariel in Great Britain.

**The Junior**

Adler's entry into the scooter market came with the Junior. This was powered by a fan-cooled 98cc (50x50mm) two-stroke engine producing 3.75bhp and operating through a three-speed foot-change gearbox. At 44mph (71km/h) the top speed was very similar to the DKW Hobby. And like the latter, for its engine size the Junior was a comparatively large machine. If nothing else, its 14in wheels proved its designer was more used to motor cycles than scooters, even if Adler claimed that the 'long stretched double swinging arm gear and large wheels ensure truly ideal roadholding'. The brochure blurb continued, 'The power and economy of the proven Adler engine [developed from the motor cycle unit], its quick starting [it had an electric start as standard], easy hill climbing and steady perseverance on the motor highway can be taken for granted and need hardly be mentioned at all.'

Although the Junior sold well both at home and abroad what it really needed was a larger engine. A 125 version was built, but never left the prototype stage.

The Junior continued until 1957, even though motor cycle production had been axed a few months earlier due to the massive downturn in German motor cycle sales. Then the giant Grundig Corporation acquired a controlling interest in Adler and, shortly afterwards, senior management were instructed to concentrate their efforts solely upon typewriter production.

**Triumph and Hercules**

Just as the British Triumph marque built a scooter with BSA, the German Triumph (known as TWN in certain export markets) did the same with Hercules.

The scooter in question was the TWN Contessa/Hercules R200. The first public viewing of the TWN Contessa came at the Brussels Show in January 1955. The Contessa used the 197cc split-single two-stroke engine (2x45x62mm) from the TWN Cornet motor cycle, but suitably modified for its new function by having fan-cooling, an electric start and 12-volt Noris electrical equipment. Suspension was by leading arm front forks and a swinging arm shock absorber at the rear.

The TWN Contessa was sold in Great Britain as the Prior Viscount from 1958, built under licence by BP Scooters of Wolverhampton.

Although sharing virtually identical body-work, the Hercules R200, which made its début at the 1956 Frankfurt Show, was powered by a Sachs 191cc (65x68mm) conventional single-cylinder piston-port induction two-stroke engine with four speeds, producing 10.2bhp at 5,250rpm.

Early in 1957, the R200 was imported into Great Britain by Cyril Kieft & Co Ltd, and after October that year by BP Scooters. In 1958, the importers changed again, this time to Industria of London. None of the Hercules version were sold under this brand name in Great Britain because the name could not be used as it was owned by Raleigh

*DKW's Hobby featured infinitely variable automatic transmission by belt.*

Industries, makers of Raleigh cycles, mopeds – and scooters (*see* Chapter 4). So under the Kieft regime the scooter was known as a Prior, the name of the importer, but in Great Britain it was not available until February 1956, when a batch was imported by Industria of Berkshire.

The Hercules/Sachs-engined machine outlived the Triumph original, the last of the latter being manufactured in 1957, whereas the former continued until 1964.

The German Triumph Company also built the ill-fated Tessy, powered by a 125cc Sachs engine, but this proved a commercial disaster.

From 1964, Hercules manufactured 50cc KTM Scooters under licence from the Austrian firm.

## Victoria

Founded in Nuremburg by Max Frankenburger and Max Offenstein, the Victoria bicycle works began trading in 1886. After thirteen successful years, the company switched from muscle power to the internal combustion engine.

Victoria began by fitting single-cylinder Zedal and Fafnir power units into frames of its own design. These machines were sold until 1918, but after the Great War production concentrated on 493cc motor cycles with horizontally opposed twin-cylinder engines manufactured by BMW.

In 1923 BMW decided to build complete motor cycles and Victoria engaged BMW's former designer, Martin Stolle. Stolle only stayed for a couple of years, so Victoria later used engines designed by Albert Roder and Richard Küchen.

After 1945, Victoria re-entered motor cycle production with a series of two-stroke utility motor cycles plus the 347cc *Bergmeister* (mountain master) overhead-valve twin, the latter also the work of Richard Küchen.

Victoria also built and sold the Nicky

micro-scooter powered by a 48cc (38x42mm) two-stroke engine.

During 1956 Victoria hit financial trouble. An attempt was made to improve flagging sales by entering into an agreement with the Italian Parilla Company (*see* Chapter 2), but ultimately this bore no fruit and eventually, in 1958, Victoria was one of three companies (the others being DKW and Express) that amalgamated to form the Zweirad Union.

## The Peggy

The International Frankfurt Show in October 1953 saw Victoria launch a scooter called the Peggy. This was not only luxurious but practical, with excellent weather protection and a lusty 198cc (65x60mm)

*A period DKW Hobby publicity photograph promoting its use for transporting its owner to go hunting and fishing!*

single-cylinder two-stroke engine with a power output of 10bhp. Production, however, did not commence fully until a year later. An interesting technical innovation of the Peggy (shared with the Victoria Swing motor cycles) was its push-button gear change mechanism.

The wheels were large for a scooter at 16in, while suspension was taken care of by leading link front forks and a swinging arm at the rear.

## DKW

The story of this great marque began with the birth in 1898 of Jorgen Skaffe Rasmussen in Nakskow, Denmark. The young Rasmussen moved to Dusseldorf, Germany in 1904 and then, in 1907, to Zschopau in Saxony.

Rasmussen began trading in 1919 and thanks to the engineering skills of men like Hugo Ruppe became a world leader in the development of the two-stroke engine.

Besides motor cycles, DKW also built scooter-like machines: the 122cc Golem (1921) and the 142cc Lamos (1922). But although both offered armchair comfort, they were unsuccessful sellers. Not so the various motor cycles, and by 1931 DKW could claim to be the world's largest motor cycle manufacturer, retaining a major presence in the industry until the end of the Second World War. Then, with its works overrun by the Soviets, DKW was reformed at Ingoldstadt in West Germany.

DKW's first post-war production motor cycle was the RT125, which made its début in 1949. With the arrival of the 1950s, so came success in both sales and competitions, with DKW claiming many victories in road racing, motocross and long distance trials.

### The Hobby
In September 1954, DKW entered the scooter world with a 74cc (47x45mm) single-cylinder two-stroke – the Hobby. This was a highly innovative design featuring automatic transmission, using an elaborate system of belts with a clutch disengaging the gears. Many scooter riders were none too keen on the motor cycle feature of the kick-starter, so the DKW engineering team opted for what is best described as the 'lawn mower' image, thanks to a pull-starter, positioned next to the rider's left foot.

Although it only put out 3bhp at 5,000rpm, the Hobby still reached 40mph (64km/h). It also had the advantage of looking like a full-size scooter of at least 150cc, but costing considerably less to purchase and run. According to test figures obtained by *Motor Cycling*, fuel consumption was 139mpg (2ltr/100km) at a steady 25mph (40km/h). To simplify matters for the user, an automatic petroil mixer was located in the fuel tank. A trend by some other manufacturers towards larger wheels for scooters had been followed by the adoption of 16in rims shod with 2.50 section tyres. Front suspension was by an undamped telescopic fork, whilst the rear wheel was mounted on a pivoted fork controlled by rubber in compression.

By mid-1956 DKW was, like many other German motor cycle manufacturers, experiencing financial troubles, and by the end of that year the Hobby was taken out of production after some 40,000 machines had been manufactured.

However the Hobby lived on, thanks to a licence agreement entered into earlier with the French company Manurhin, who also carried out several modifications of their own. These included updating the styling, an increase in engine size, wider section tyres and improving the automatic gear change, the latter being the source of a new name – the Beltomatic.

*Variable Drive*
The automatic transmission provided an infinitely variable drive between top and bottom ratios of 8.33 and 24.4:1 via a system

# The Puch Alpine

The SR and SRA Alpine series, which made their début in 1957 with a 150 class engine and new bodywork, were developed from the company's RL and RLA models.

Like German scooters, Austrian models were very over-engineered, but proved exceptionally reliable and long-lived, 'quality first' being Puch's byword as regards its Alpine scooter. The design, finish and workmanship were all first class, with several unusual and interesting features.

The steering and road holding qualities were excellent, even by motor cycle standards, whilst Brian Smith writing for *Motor Cycle Mechanic* in its May 1962 issue described the brakes as 'fantastic'.

Machines gave the rider confidence right from the first time he or she sat astride an Alpine. And it wasn't just the steering, road holding and brakes – the detail that had gone into the design was just as outstanding. For example, the lighting switches (including the headlamp flasher) were very neat and well positioned, whilst there seemed to be a fuse for everything. The lights themselves were exceptional for a scooter of the era – even the stop light was really bright. This of course was helped on the SRA version by its twin batteries, providing 12 volts for the electric starter.

The engine, a single-cylinder piston-port two-stroke had a displacement of 147cc (57x57mm) and produced 6bhp at 5,500rpm. It was a rugged unit. However, the Achilles heel of the Alpine was that its three-speed gearbox suffered badly from clutch drag, particularly when cold. Again, according to Brian Smith of *Motor Cycle Mechanic*, 'I was not able to cure this and therefore all gear changes were rather noisy … I do not like the twist-grip gear changes, but the Puch is better than most, being very positive in action.'

A feature of the Puch scooters was that the entire bodywork (including the seats and spare wheel if fitted), hinged up from the rear. There were also three 'door-sections', giving access to the twin batteries, the comprehensive original equipment tool kit, the fuel tap and carburettor tickler.

Amongst the outstanding detail points was the inclusion of a grease gun as standard, a neat lifting handle, a steering lock, a unique choke operation, a luggage hook and an easily read speedometer.

With a maximum speed of 58mph (93km/h), the SRA 150 Alpine was considerably quicker than the Lambretta Li150.

As Brian Smith concluded at the end of the test, 'Here is a machine for beginner or enthusiast alike. It is simple to handle, safe, and easily maintained. At the same time it sets standards of design and workmanship which are well above average, at a price below average.'

| Specification | 1961 Puch SR150 Alpine |
|---|---|
| Engine | Air-cooled, two-stroke, single |
| Displacement | 147cc |
| Bore & stroke | 57x57mm |
| Gearbox | Three-speed, twist-grip change |
| Wheel size | 12in |
| Power | 6bhp |
| Maximum speed | 58mph (93km/h) |

*The Alpine was imported into Great Britain by Ryders Autoservice of Liverpool from the late 1950s until the mid-1960s.*

*The finish of the Alpine was first class which, together with several unusual features, made it an interesting addition to the scooter ranks. Only its poor three-speed twistgrip gear change and heavy clutch action let it down.*

of belts. Because of its unusual nature I feel it is worth explaining this in some detail.

On the engine shaft was an expanding pulley, operated by a centrifugal governor built into its centre hub, which pulley drove a second, spring-loaded pulley on a countershaft through a vee-belt. From there a helical gear connected the countershaft to a sprocket that provided the final drive to the rear wheel by chain. Any increase in engine speed resulting from opening the throttle or meeting a down gradient caused the engine shaft pulley flanges to close up, thus raising the gear ratio, while the spring loading of the countershaft pulley maintained the correct belt tension. Conversely, as the engine speed fell, the gear ratio was automatically lowered to suit conditions.

Operating a handlebar-mounted lever disengaged the drive by separating the flanges of the engine shaft pulley – effectively acting as a combined clutch and bottom gear. But with a bottom ratio as low as 24.4:1, this was in most cases necessary only for stopping and starting. A neutral position was provided by means of a lever that disconnected the drive by fully expanding the engine shaft pulley.

### The Standard and The *Luxus*
Two versions of the Hobby were marketed – Standard and *Luxus* (de Luxe). The main difference between the two was that the *Luxus* was fitted with a full-width front hub and had a pillion saddle, whereas for the standard model this item was an extra. Finish was also more lavish on the *Luxus*, with additional chrome-work and wheel grilles, together with passenger grab handles on the rear cowling.

*In Retrospect*
We already know that a major downturn in two-wheeled sales during the late 1950s was caused by the improving economic position of the West German population, and this was why so many German scooters were eventually exported.

Another less well-known factor that affected domestic scooter sales was that the government eventually outlawed scooters from the *Autobahn* network, which ultimately led to their decline as a serious form of transportation for German citizens.

## The Austrian Industry

Although relatively small compared with its neighbour Germany, Austria was still able to boast of Puch, a sizable scooter manufacturer.

Prior to the Great War of 1914, Austria had ruled large parts of Europe, the Austro-Hungarian Empire's only real political rivals being Great Britain and France. After defeat in 1918, Austria was divested of some of its former territory and Puch was left as the only internationally known Austrian motor cycle manufacturer.

The aftermath of Second World War saw more changes and although Puch continued in its dominant position, two new important names emerged – KTM and engine specialists Rotax.

## Puch

Puch joined the ranks of the world's scooter manufacturers in 1952 with the launch of two machines, the R and RL. Both were powered by a single-cylinder two-stroke engine. But unlike the Puch motor cycles of the era, the new scooter had a single piston, rather than the famous Puch split single (two-piston) design. The scooter engine displaced 121cc, with bore and stroke dimensions of 52x57mm, producing 4.5bhp at 5,100rpm. Other features included a three-speed twist-grip-controlled gearbox and 12in wheels with 3.25 section tyres. A notable difference between the otherwise very similar machines was that the R version had a flywheel magneto, whereas the RL featured battery/coil ignition.

In 1954, Puch sold the RL model to the

Swiss Condor Company, as well as developing a three-wheeler with two rear wheels driven by a differential. Puch axed the R version in 1955, but the RL continued, to be joined by the RLA that had an electric start and twin 12-volt batteries.

## The Alpine

Next, in 1957, came the famous Alpine scooter, today the best remembered of all Austrian models. The 147cc engine was a development of the 125cc unit (by increasing the bore size to 57mm). It is worth pointing out that all Puch scooters were of the highest quality. The Alpine models offered excellent steering, road holding and brakes, whilst there was a hinged rear cover providing access to the engine. Alpine models were coded ST and SRA, the latter featuring an electric start and 12-volt ignition.

By November 1964, the British Puch importers, Ryders Auto Service of Liverpool, listed three scooters: the 60cc Cheetah at £109 10s; the 60cc Pony at £117 17s 6d; and the 150cc Alpine at £182, the British Alpine being the SRA with an electric start.

## KTM

KTM (Kronreif, Trunkenpolz and Mattinghofen – the names of the two founders and the factory's location) produced its first machine, a 98cc motor cycle in 1953.

In its early days KTM built a number of scooters and lightweight motor cycles powered by Sachs-Rotax two-stroke engines.

The first scooter arrived in 1956, the 150cc Mirabell, and was very much a de luxe Germanic design. The following year, 1957, saw the début of the 49cc, three-speed Mecky moped-scooter. But the real success story for KTM in the scooter field came in 1960 with the new Pony model, which featured ultra-modern styling: twin car-type headlamps set close together at the top of the front apron, a

two-tone dual seat, whitewall tyres and extensive bodywork incorporating tail fins! The Pony was also built under licence by the German firm Gritzner-Kayser.

By the mid-1960s KTM had begun to switch its production to off-road competition motorcycles.

## Lohner

The third Austrian scooter manufacturer was the Lohner firm based in Vienna. Lohner were the first Austrian firm to build a scooter, the L98T arriving during 1951 powered by a 98cc German Sachs two-stroke engine, with a two-speed gearbox.

Then, in 1953, Lohner went upmarket with the L200 *Super Roller* (super scooter), powered by a Rotax 199cc (62x66mm) unit, which produced 8.3bhp at 5,000rpm and drove through a Famo four-speed gearbox. Wheel size was 10in with 4.00 section tyres.

For the 1956 season, Lohner created two new scooters, the Rapid 125 and 200. The smaller-engined machine utilized a Sachs power unit, while the 200 used an Ilo motor. The Rapid 200 was also offered with an integral sidecar constructed into the bodywork of the scooter.

Finally, in 1957, Lohner produced the strangely named (well would you buy a machine with this name?) Sissy, very much a combination of scooter, motor cycle and moped with a 49cc Sachs engine and three speeds.

## Quality Products

German and Austrian scooters shared that Germanic quality, which was somehow never of quite the same standard in other countries' machines – certainly, in comparison with mainstream Italian brands. They were almost over-engineered. However, as owners will tell you, this paid off in terms of reliability and pride of ownership.

# 4   Great Britain

Compared with Italy, West Germany and even Japan, the British scooter industry was both fragmented and, in the case of the major motor cycle manufacturers, much too late on the scene. Even so it produced some notably interesting designs and a few real oddballs.

## Excelsior

At the end of the Second World War in 1945, the British government, then in desperate need of American dollars, sold off its stock of Excelsior Welbike ex-army scooters (that had been designed for dropping by parachute in a container!) to Gimbels, a large department store in New York. The *New York Herald Tribune* dated Sunday 9 December 1946, carried a story concerning the shipment. In March that year, asked if any surplus British Army Welbike machines would be released for domestic civilian sales, the government Minister of Supply John Wilmot replied that all surpluses of these machines had been disposed of to an export firm for resale in the USA!

## Brockhouse

Due to demand for a civilian version of the Welbike, the Corgi was put into production in 1947 by Brockhouse Engineering of

*The Corgi (a Mark II is seen here) came about due to the demand for a civilian version of the wartime Welbike and was produced by Brockhouse from November 1947 onwards.*

Lancashire. By November of that year, having been previously marketed exclusively for export, Brockhouse announced that supplies would be released for the transport-starved home market, and that Jack Olding of West London had been appointed sole distributor for Great Britain and Northern Ireland.

Confusingly, the original Excelsior-made Welbike had used a Villiers engine, whereas the Brockhouse Corgi was fitted with an Excelsior

# 3 Primaries.

**A GENERAL UTILITY VEHICLE**

**THE QUICKEST WAY TO DELIVER THE GOODS**

**PUBLIC SERVICE**

This page is printed in four colours—the colours are obtained by superimposing the three primaries —Yellow, Red and Blue. The result is a practically unlimited range of colour.

The three suggestions shewn for the use of the Gadabout may likewise be called "primaries," superimposed upon the individual needs of the owner they, too, provide an almost unlimited range of usefulness.

Whatever the daily task, or common round, it can be brightened up with the Swallow Gadabout.

## the Swallow Gadabout

**SOLO** *brightens up the daily round* **COMMERCIAL** *delivers the goods*

Giving over 95 miles per gallon the Gadabout is equipped with the Villiers 10 D. 122 c.c. two-stroke engine, 3-speed gear box, has a cruising speed of 30 m.p.h., comfortable seating and maximum weather protection. Ask also for details of the Commercial Model equipped with a Box Capacity of 11 Cubic Feet, with a Maximum Payload of 2 cwt., offering a solution to numerous economical delivery problems. Obtainable from all authorised Swallow dealers.

**SWALLOW COACHBUILDING CO (1935) LTD.**
*THE AIRPORT · WALSALL · STAFFORDSHIRE · ENGLAND*

*The Swallow Gadabout was another early post-war British scooter. It was powered by a Villiers 122cc 10D two-stroke engine.*

Spryt unit. Both were single-cylinder two-strokes of 98cc displacement, with a horizontal cylinder and countershaft clutch.

A kick-start and sidecar platform were soon fitted to the Corgi, whilst in 1949 two speeds and telescopic forks were available as options, these becoming a standard fitment in 1952. Production finally ceased in 1954, by which time the Corgi had been succeeded by much improved designs from other manufacturers.

## Swallow

Swallow was formed back in the early 1920s by William, later Sir William, Lyons (of Jaguar car fame).

The first details of the all-new British scooter, the Swallow Gadabout, appeared in November 1946 – a prototype having been under test in the preceding months. With the total enclosure of its pre-war 122cc Villiers 9D engine and transmission, the Swallow Gadabout offered basic, economical transport. It featured three speeds, 8in wheels with 4.00 section tyres, the rims being of the bolted-up split type, and there was an optional light-weight commercial sidecar. This latter assembly could perhaps have been guaranteed, as the Swallow Coach Building Company was an established sidecar manufacturer. However, compared with the Italian Vespa that made its début at about the same time, the Gadabout was a pretty agricultural machine. A rigid duplex steel tube frame and a pair of undamped front forks provided little in the way of creature comforts.

A major problem of the Gadabout scooter was its extremely poor power-to-weight ratio. In 1950, a Mark II version was offered with a 122cc Villiers 10D engine, producing 4.8bhp (against 3.15bhp of the unit it replaced), whilst leading link forks with bonded rubber suspension provided a slightly better ride.

Then, at the end of 1950, the Major, a commercial three-wheeler, based on the Gadabout, made its bow. This was powered by a 197cc Villiers engine with a four-bladed cooling fan replacing the two-blade type of the Gadabout.

However, by 1952 Swallow had quit the scene, returning to its core business of building sidecars.

## Velocette

Velocette was one of the most famous of all British motor cycle brand names. The first motor cycles appeared in 1905 under the Veloce name. It was not until 1913, with the début of the firm's first two-stroke model, that the name Velocette was used. During the inter-war years, Velocette often led the world in both racing and innovative design, thanks to engineers such as Harold Willis, Phil Irving and Charles Udall.

Post-war, although Velocette produced some well-known models, it struggled financially. This was not helped by its largely failed attempts to move away from sporting motor cycles to more 'bread-and-butter' designs, including the Viceroy scooter, which made its début in 1960.

### The LE

Someone once described Velocette's LE (little engine) as, 'Great Britain's finest scooter'. But like Italy's Moto Guzzi *Galletto* (*see* Chapter 2), the LE was, strictly speaking, part motor cycle, part scooter.

This technically interesting and innovative design made its first public bow towards the end of 1948, but the idea had been around for some time, the Australian designer Phil Irving having drawn out the original concept as long ago as 1942.

With the LE, the Birmingham firm discarded all perceived ideas of what should constitute a motor cycle, and instead set about the task of translating an engine, transmission and final drive into a single 'mono' assembly,

*The Velocette LE was designed for the very same role as the scooter – economical transport with excellent rider protection. This photograph dates from the launch of the original 150 version in late 1948.*

regardless of the type of frame to be used, and not relying upon this to hold all the bits and pieces together. The aim was to produce a powered two-wheeler for 'Mr Everyman' (this theory being fully embraced by Velocette director Eugene Goodman), which could provide continuous service over many thousands of miles without attention; a machine that answered the various criticisms that previously had been levelled at conventional motor cycles; a machine suitable for every class of road condition and one that could be ridden in all weathers in which two-wheeled travel was reasonably possible without special clothing being necessary. In fact, just the requirements for a scooter!

The LE Mark 1 had a 149cc (44x49mm) liquid-cooled horizontally opposed twin-cylinder engine with a three-speed hand-change gearbox. Both the primary and final drives were by gears (the latter together with a shaft). The main backbone of the LE frame was

a 22-gauge sheet-steel pressing, the steering head being a bolted-up assembly.

In 1951 the engine size was increased to 192cc (50x49mm), and for the 1958 season, with the introduction of the Mark III, a four-speed gearbox was added, and a switch made to conventional foot gearchange operation.

By mid-1964 approximately 30,000 LEs had been produced in some fifteen years and it now featured 12-volt electrics – a direct result of its widespread use by numerous British police forces. Production finally ended in 1971 at the same time as Velocette's demise.

## The Italian Invasion

As detailed in Chapter 2, by the early 1950s the Italians in the shape of Vespa and Lambretta were dominating the scooter scene all across Europe – including Great Britain. The Bristol-based Douglas concern had secured a licence agreement with Piaggio to build Vespas in

*A Velocette advertisement proclaiming the virtues of the LE, including a flat-twin four-stroke engine, shaft final drive, and front and rear suspension – plus comfort, economy and silence.*

# The Velocette Viceroy

As explained in the main text, if one discounts the LE, the Velocette scooter project lasted for much of the 1950s. But unfortunately, the end product, the Viceroy, did not actually arrive until the end of 1960 and in retrospect this was far too late, as the market for large, luxury scooters by this time had all but disappeared. The German scooter industry had already mopped up what sales there were to be had in this sector, with models such as the Maicoletta, the Dürkopp Diana, the NSU *Prima* V and the Zündapp 200 Bella. With a mere 582 examples sold, the Viceroy is now generally held responsible for the ultimate demise of Velocette.

All this is unfortunate, as in many ways the Velocette scooter was an advanced design with an outstanding performance, with only the styling being a source of criticism. Scooter historian Mike Webster commented, 'The Viceroy style may be questionable but its mechanical integrity and fitness for purpose as a long-distance, high-speed cruiser can not be faulted.'

The centre of any machine is its engine – and in the Viceroy's case this was especially true. As one commentator said at its launch, 'The power unit and transmission bristles with novelty', just two examples of this being that the crankpins were spaced at 180 degrees to provide near-perfect balance (meaning both cylinders fired together), which was an almost unique feature for a European engine, and certainly not one to be found in a scooter at that time, and the use of automatic reed inlet valves. And of course it was the first two-stroke from Velocette since production of the GTP motor cycle ceased at the end of the 1930s.

Both cylinder heads and barrels were of light alloy; as for the reeds themselves, these were thin, stainless steel devices. The crankcases split vertically; each of the oval-section connecting rods featured two rows of caged big-end rollers, but the small-ends were unusual in making use of Torrington needle-roller bearings – a feature adopted with petroil lubrication in mind. The rotor for the Lucas 60-watt alternator was keyed to the front of the crankshaft. A car-type Lucas electric starter motor operated a large toothed ring on the flywheel. A four-speed gearbox was mounted adjacent to the rear wheel hub. So comprising the chain-reduction assembly, gearbox and bevel box, the entire transmission pivoted from its forward end. With reduction gear sprockets, the clutch ran at just under half-engine speed.

*Even though few were sold, the Viceroy was in many ways an excellent design. Its only two major failings were its styling and the fact that it was years too late, not going on sale until the end of 1960.*

*The centre of any machine is its engine, and the Viceroy power unit bristled with technical interest, including its 248cc flat twin layout, reed-valve induction and crankpins spaced at 180 degrees to provide near perfect balance. Note also the interesting frame layout.*

With the exception of its backbone shape, the Viceroy's all-welded frame was reasonably conventional – at least by motor cycle, if not scooter standards – being of circular steel tubing, bent through ninety degrees.

However, because the engine was underslung, the tube did not drop so deeply from the steering head as might have been expected. To this main tubular backbone were welded the various support brackets. Half a dozen steel pressings made up the bodywork.

Other cycle part components included undamped telescopic front forks, 6in brake drums, an aluminium casing that acted as an instrument holder for the speedometer, an ammeter and separate light and ignition switches.

The 248cc (54x54mm) air-cooled twin-cylinder engine put out 18bhp at 5,000rpm, giving the 302lb (137kg) Viceroy a maximum speed of 70mph (113km/h). Acceleration was brisk, whilst the reed-valve induction system contributed in no small way towards the Viceroy giving both economy and smooth running.

Velocette's design chief Charles Udall was in charge of the machine's development. But in fairness it was the directors of the company who were largely responsible for the overlong pre-birth stage. The actual engine was completed in 1957, but the Viceroy was not announced until the end of 1960 and then did not go on sale until 1961.

Not only this, but initial thoughts earlier in the 1950s had been centred around a water-cooled scooter developed from the LE, but this was ultimately shelved in favour of starting from scratch in order to produce what was hoped would be a truly unique machine. In that, the Viceroy certainly lived up to its creator's hopes. However, it failed on other grounds. These included the purchase price, weight and bulk. But most of all it was not only too late, but it was what a motor cycle designer thought a scooter should be, rather than the successful proven formula of machines such as the best-selling Italian Lambretta and Vespa models.

Having tooled up for a production run of thousands, Velocette ended up with a financial disaster on its hands. With a negligible home market and only the odd private export sale, it is absolutely certain that the Viceroy greatly accelerated the downfall of the Velocette marque.

# VICEROY

1st. MARCH 1961

## PRICE LIST

**Velocette "VICEROY" Scooter**

| Basic Price | Purchase Tax | | Total |
|---|---|---|---|
| £164 2 10 | £33 17 2 | | £198 0 0 |

### ACCESSORIES FOR THE "VICEROY" SCOOTER

| DESCRIPTION | FINISH | PRICE |
|---|---|---|
| Parcel Hook | | 8 6 |
| Mirror ... ... ... ... | ... | 17 6 |
| Front Wheel Embellishers ... ... | Set | £2 2 0 |
| Luggage Carrier ... ... ... | Enamelled | £5 5 0 |
| Luggage Carrier ... ... ... | Plated | £7 15 0 |
| Screen and Fittings ... ... ... | | £5 15 0 |
| 4 Leg 12" "Octopus" Luggage Strap ... ... ... ... | ... | 8 0 |
| Seat Cover ... ... ... | Tartan | £1 7 6 |
| Direction Indicators ... ... | ... | £7 19 0 |
| | | (inc. £1 7s. 2d. P.T.) |
| Lycett "Triple Suite" Pannier Bag and Frame only ... ... | Each | £2 13 6 |
| | | (inc. 7s. 6d. P.T.) |
| Lycett "Triple Suite" Case only ... | ... | £2 12 0 |
| | | (inc. 6s. 2d. P.T.) |
| Lycett "Triple Suite" Luggage (2 Panniers, 1 Case, 2 Frames) | Tartan | £7 12 6 |
| | | (inc. 18s. 11d. P.T.) |
| Fixing Bolts and Washers for "Triple Suite" ... ... | ... | 8 6 |

The Pannier Frames are integral with the Luggage Carrier which has, therefore, to be fitted if Panniers are ordered.

### PRICES ARE SUBJECT TO ALTERATION WITHOUT NOTICE

VELOCE LIMITED
YORK ROAD, HALL GREEN, BIRMINGHAM, 28

10M. 1631

*A Viceroy price list dated 1 March 1961, including not just the scooter itself, but also the accessories.*

| Specification | 1961 Velocette Viceroy |
|---|---|
| Engine | Air-cooled, two-stroke (reed-valve), horizontal twin |
| Displacement | 248cc |
| Bore & stroke | 54x54mm |
| Gearbox | Four-speed, foot-change |
| Wheel size | 12in |
| Power | 15bhp |
| Maximum speed | 70mph (113km/h) |

Great Britain, first displaying an imported Vespa at the 1949 London Earls Court Show, with Douglas launching its own Vespa range on 15 March 1951. It should be explained that many of the Douglas Vespas had British components such as carburettors, electrical components, saddles, tyres and several other items.

Although never built under licence in Great Britain, the Lambretta range was imported in large numbers from the early 1950s onwards.

## The British Response

Except for the Welbike, Corgi and Gadabout, the British scooter effort was, in the main, exceedingly slow in getting off the ground. And some, like the Velocette LE and the Bond Minibyke that arrived in early 1950, defied an accurate description of whether they were in fact motor cycles or scooters. The LE, with its water-cooled flat-twin side-valve engine, comprehensive enclosure and weather protection for the rider, had large (19in) wheels that placed it in the motor cycle domain.

However, the Bond Minibyke defied either motor cycle or scooter tagging. Designed by Lawrence Bond (of the Bond minicar three-wheeler fame), it had an all-aluminium frame manufactured from sheet rolled into a large tube from which the engine hung, with mudguards that enclosed the majority of both 16in wheels. At first the engine was a 98cc Villiers, but in 1951 it was replaced by a 125cc JAP two-stroke. Production ceased in 1953.

## BAC

Bond Aircraft & Engineering (BAC) created its Gazelle scooter in spring 1952 with a 122cc Villiers 10D two-stroke power unit and 4.00x8 tyres. Later that year, a second Gazelle was produced, this time with a 98cc IF Villiers unit. By 1953, the rights to the Gazelle were sold to the Projects & Developments Company, and

*A 1952 Douglas-Vespa advertisement.*

although it concentrated its production on the micro-car, it continued scooter production until 1962.

## The PI, 2, 3 & 4

Lawrence Bond returned to scooters in January 1958, with the launch of his Pl,

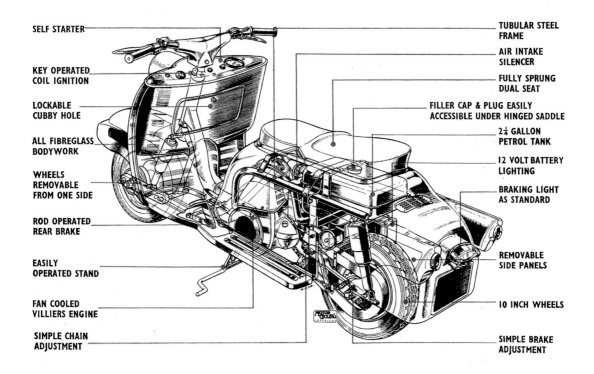

SELF STARTER

KEY OPERATED
COIL IGNITION

LOCKABLE
CUBBY HOLE

ALL FIBREGLASS
BODYWORK

WHEELS
REMOVABLE
FROM ONE SIDE

ROD OPERATED
REAR BRAKE

EASILY
OPERATED STAND

FAN COOLED
VILLIERS ENGINE

SIMPLE CHAIN
ADJUSTMENT

TUBULAR STEEL
FRAME

AIR INTAKE
SILENCER

FULLY SPRUNG
DUAL SEAT

FILLER CAP & PLUG EASILY
ACCESSIBLE UNDER HINGED SADDLE

2½ GALLON
PETROL TANK

12 VOLT BATTERY
LIGHTING

BRAKING LIGHT
AS STANDARD

REMOVABLE
SIDE PANELS

10 INCH WHEELS

SIMPLE BRAKE
ADJUSTMENT

*A brochure illustration showing a cutaway view of the new-for-1958, Bond P1, powered by a fan-cooled 31C Villiers 148cc engine with an electric start. The chassis was innovative, as it used the engine as a stressed member of the frame.*

powered by a Villiers 148cc Mark 31C/35F three-speed fan-cooled engine, and equipped with a Siba starter/generator. The frame was of all-welded tubular-steel construction, with the engine employed as a stressed member (very unusual in the scooter world at that time). There was swinging fork suspension at both ends, each with a single hydraulic unit. The P1's bodywork was manufactured in fibreglass and incorporated tail fins and portholes. It is worth noting that Lawrence Bond had gained experience with this material with his Berkeley car bodies and the P1 was one of the very first scooters to use a fibreglass body.

In July 1958, a more powerful version of the

Bond scooter was put into production. Known as the P2, this was similar to the P1 except that the body was fitted with a more powerful Villiers 197cc Mark 9E fan-cooled engine with a four-speed gearbox. A Siba starter was again a standard fitment.

In 1960, the 147cc P3 and 197cc P4 replaced the earlier P1/P2 designs. These were equipped with a new frame that mounted the engine's lower to provide a superior centre of gravity. The bodywork was now much more curvaceous, giving a modern and graceful appearance.

Bond continued scooter production until 1962.

*A 1957 dealer advertisement for the Piatti. However, it was not quite 'All British' as claimed.*

*Another British scooter with an Italian connection was the Britax Scooterette, which used a Ducati engine.*

## The Italian Influence

Besides the British-built Douglas-Vespa series and huge imports of Lambrettas direct from the Innocenti plant in Milan there were, during the early 1950s, two other Italian-influenced but far less successful scooters sold in Great Britain.

The first was a scooter designed by the London-based Italian, Vincenzo Piatti. This made its first public appearance, in prototype form, at the 35th Brussels Show in January 1952. It was eventually built in Great Britain by Cyclemaster, as well as in Belgium by *Les Anciens Establissments D'Ieteren* (Aldimi). According to Michael Dregni, 'The Piatti was quite simply one of the oddest scooters ever built. Its styling bespoke a cigar on wheels with handlebars and a seat perched precariously on top.' The vertical slat at the front of the 'cigar' bodywork was not just there for style, but to assist cooling of the 125cc, three-speed engine unit. The seat worked like that of a conventional pedal cycle, with up and down column adjustment for height.

The second British scooter with Italian connections came from the Britax Organisation, which was the original British Ducati importer. Britax built a range of models powered by the 48cc Cucciolo pull-rod

IT'S HERE!

the new all British **Dayton Albatross**

An amazing, brand-new machine

designed to give you

**HIGHER CRUISING SPEEDS**

**GREATER STABILITY**

**MUCH MORE COMFORT**

**GREATER RELIABILITY**

than any similar machine!

*see it at the Show*

*STAND 171*

*make a point of inspecting the new Earles fork*

Dayton Cycle Company Ltd., London, N.W.10

DC2

*Dayton was a long-established bicycle manufacturer which launched its Albatross luxury scooter at the beginning of November 1954, to coincide with its 50th anniversary.*

engine, including the Hurricane racer and the Scooterette, both of which appeared in 1955. But neither of these models was a commercial success, and Britax returned to producing motor accessories from 1956 onwards.

## Dayton

Dayton was a long-established bicycle manufacturer. Its only foray into powered two-wheelers, prior to its scooter involvement, had come in 1939 with a 98cc Villiers-powered autocycle.

It announced its Albatross luxury scooter at the beginning of November 1954, to coincide with the 50th anniversary of the company. Weighing in at 280lb (127kg), the newcomer was initially powered by the 225cc Villiers Mark 1H two-stroke single-cylinder engine with a four-speed gearbox in the unit. The front fork was a Reynolds-Earles pivoted assembly, with swinging arm rear suspension. Woodhead-Monroe spring and hydraulic

damper units were employed, a pair at both front and rear. A single 2in (50mm) diameter tube formed the main frame, the bodywork being of pressed steel, whilst the brake drums were manufactured of bi-metal Al-Fin with finning to aid cooling.

Owing to delays in the delivery of certain components, the Albatross did not enter production until May 1955. Then in 1957, the Albatross Twin was added, with twin-cylinder 249cc Villiers 2T power. The following year the front fork's assembly was ditched in favour of a more conventional telescopic unit. In addition, the model names were revised, the Albatross becoming the Empire, whilst the T was renamed the Continental. Then, at the end of October 1958, a light, smaller capacity scooter was added. Named the Flamingo, this was powered by a 173cc Villiers 2L/35F engine, with three speeds and a Siba starter-generator. The frame and bodywork were shared in a joint venture with Panther and Sun.

*A large percentage of the British scooter industry, including Bond, Dayton, DKR and Phoenix, fitted Villiers-made engines as standard equipment.*

an unusual design, each fork arm consisting of a thin, mild steel plate in the shape of a right-angled triangle, the plates being bridged at the pivot point. Two coil-spring suspension units were employed, which lay parallel to the frame and attached to the fork arms at right angles; capped rods passing through the middle compressed the springs when the suspension was loaded. Wheel size was 8in with 3.50 section tyres.

The Phoenix 150 scooter made its public début at the Earls Court Show later that year. By the following year's show, in November 1957, three new models were shown: the 150 de Luxe, the Phoenix 200 and the T – a 250 twin powered by a 249 Villiers 2T with Siba dynastart. The basic design of the de Luxe was the same as the existing standard model, including the 30C engine unit.

In May 1958 four new models replaced the existing line-up, all with new fibreglass body-work. These were the 150 Super de Luxe, the S150, the S200 and the T250. Fan-cooling was found on all four, with twin fans on the twin-cylinder model. The styling was considerably improved over the original range. The top-of-the-range 249cc T250 was priced at £229 17s including British purchase tax.

Later still came a pair of electric-start Villiers 324cc 3T twin-cylinder models with 17bhp at 5,800rpm.

Phoenix production ended in 1964.

## Newcomers Galore

1957–58 saw many newcomers to the British scooter manufacturing scene, including, amongst others, BSA, DMW, DKR, Triumph, Progress, and Sun.

## BSA

The giant BSA group had displayed two entirely different scooters at the London Show in November 1955. Both were the work of

## Phoenix

In July 1956 another Villiers-powered British scooter, the Phoenix, was announced in proto-type form. The power unit was a Mark 30C 147cc with a three-speed rocking pedal foot-control and a crankshaft-mounted fan. Front suspension was by a single leading link – the stanchion was of inverted L-shape and fabricated from 14-gauge steel tubing. Of pivoted-fork pattern, the rear suspension was

*Shown in prototype form at the London Earls Court Show in November 1955, the BSA Beeza scooter, with its four-stroke 198cc engine, four-speed gearbox and electric start, should have been a huge sales success, but BSA never put it into production.*

Bert Hopwood and were aimed at two entirely different markets. The 70cc (45x44mm) Dandy was 'cheap to buy and cheap to run' whilst the 198cc side-valve Beeza was, according to Hopwood, expected to be 'nearly three times the price and probably as expensive as an ordinary lightweight roadster motor cycle'.

The Beeza remained a prototype-only venture, BSA probably being put off by the 'It's wonderful, but will never sell' brigade. But for the record, the Beeza appeared to be a much better machine than the simply awful Dandy (I know, I rode one when they were new…). The Beeza offered a powerful four-stroke engine with an electric start, comfortable suspension and full, smoothly styled enclosure; whilst the transmission was by shaft to the rear wheel. The engine itself pivoted so that the expense and complication of a universal joint was avoided. There were two silencers in tandem, making the Beeza exceptionally quiet. The price quoted at the Show was £204 12s.

All in all, the Beeza seemed a certainty for success. In fact the *Motor Cycle* Show issue dated 24 November 1955 reported, 'Factory production will not be in full swing for several months yet. Meanwhile, it may be significant that some foreign buyers who have placed cautious orders for the Dandy have committed themselves heavily for the Beeza.'

Just under a year later on 1 November 1956, it was reported that BSA had announced that its Beeza scooter was 'not to go into production yet awhile and will not be at the London Show'. Actually, after this, BSA simply and quietly forgot about its luxury scooter.

Meanwhile, the Dandy 70 had gone on sale at £74.18s. As on the prototype, the 2-speed gearbox was of the pre-selector type, gears being selected by rotation of the near-side twist-grip. The engine was mounted horizontally, with the cylinder facing rearwards. But what should have proved an excellent little runabout never made the grade, due to poor performance and suspect reliability issues.

The later joint BSA/Triumph scooter series, using either a revised Bantam 175 engine or the new 250 overhead-valve parallel twin engine that came towards the end of the 1950s, are detailed in the Triumph section (*see* page 124), these being the work of Triumph's design chief Edward Turner, rather than BSA itself, even though the two firms were part of the same industrial group.

## DMW

At the same 1955 Earls Court Show that first heralded BSA's entry into the scooter world via prototypes of the Beeza and Dandy, a much smaller British manufacturer, Dudley Motor Works (DMW), also displayed a pair of small-wheeled machines.

The first was the 98cc (47x57mm) Bambi. Like the BSA Dandy, the Bambi featured a pivoted engine-gear unit (of Villiers design), together with a fully enclosed final-drive chain. The engine, being entirely shrouded (which the BSA design was not), was fan-cooled and there was a luggage compartment under the saddle as well as a grid behind it.

The second DMW scooter was the Dumbo. Powered by a 197cc Villiers motor with an electric starter, the Dumbo had dual seats (the Bambi was a single-seater) and integral panniers. But like the BSA Beeza, the DMW Dumbo was to remain a prototype only. *Motor Cycle* had this to say: 'And another odd circumstance about the new scooters is that BSA should have called their lightweight the Dandy while DMW called theirs the Bambi. A little co-operation and pre-show consultation might have given us the far more melodious alliteration of BSA Bambi and a DMW Dandy.'

In 1961, DMW introduced the 249cc twin-cylinder Deemster scooter in standard and de luxe guises, the latter having an electric start. According to Michael Dregni, 'the Deemster resembled a motor cycle converted into a scooter, retaining the motor cycle riding position and engine placement while adding full bodywork and small diameter 12in wheels.'

Not only was a police version offered, but later examples used the Velocette Viceroy reed-valve twin-cylinder engine in place of the more usual Villiers unit.

Production finally ceased in 1967.

# DKR

Another West Midlands scooter manufacturer was the Willenhall Motor Radiator Co., a concern well known in the commercial vehicle sphere and with considerable press-work and fabricating facilities. Their range was marketed under the DKR brand name.

DKR's first offering was the Dove 147cc (55x62mm) Villiers Mark 30C three-speed engine-gear unit. A balanced, cast-alloy centrifugal fan was mounted on the rotor of

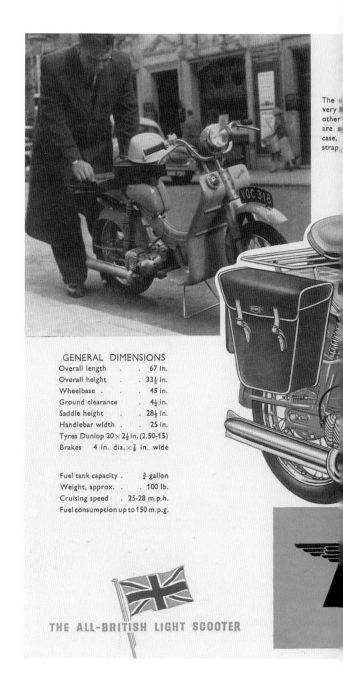

The
very
other
are s
case,
strap

**GENERAL DIMENSIONS**

| | |
|---|---|
| Overall length . . | 67 in. |
| Overall height . . | 33½ in. |
| Wheelbase . . | 45 in. |
| Ground clearance . | 4½ in. |
| Saddle height . . | 28½ in. |
| Handlebar width . . | 25 in. |
| Tyres Dunlop 20 × 2½ in. (2.50-15) | |
| Brakes 4 in. dia. × ⅞ in. wide | |
| | |
| Fuel tank capacity . | ¾ gallon |
| Weight, approx. . . | 100 lb. |
| Cruising speed . | 25-28 m.p.h. |
| Fuel consumption up to 150 m.p.g. | |

**THE ALL-BRITISH LIGHT SCOOTER**

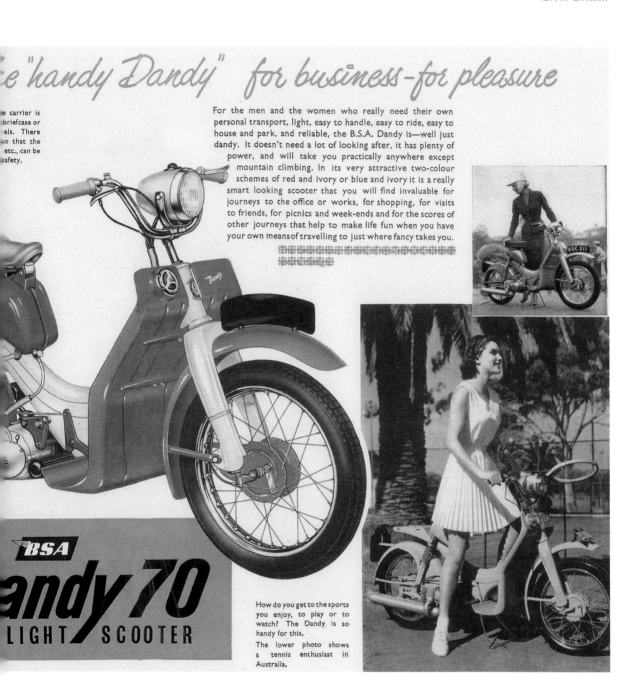

e "handy Dandy" for business–for pleasure

e carrier is
briefcase or
els. There
o that the
etc., can be
safety.

For the men and the women who really need their own personal transport, light, easy to handle, easy to ride, easy to house and park, and reliable, the B.S.A. Dandy is—well just dandy. It doesn't need a lot of looking after, it has plenty of power, and will take you practically anywhere except mountain climbing. In its very attractive two-colour schemes of red and ivory or blue and ivory it is a really smart looking scooter that you will find invaluable for journeys to the office or works, for shopping, for visits to friends, for picnics and week-ends and for the scores of other journeys that help to make life fun when you have your own means of travelling to just where fancy takes you.

**BSA**

andy 70
LIGHT SCOOTER

How do you get to the sports you enjoy, to play or to watch? The Dandy is so handy for this.
The lower photo shows a tennis enthusiast in Australia.

*BSA plumped for the Dandy 70 light scooter, which was promoted heavily, but was plagued by poor performance and suspect reliability.*

*The DKR scooter range began in 1957 with the Dove, powered by a Villiers 147cc 30C engine, but the styling was not to everyone's taste.*

the flywheel magneto and directed cooling air onto the cylinder head and barrel through sheet-steel ducting. To obtain maximum cooling, the cylinder head was turned through ninety degrees from its normal position.

Unusually and, according to DKR, to avoid having too much weight on the rear wheel, the fuel tank (in triangular shape), was carried at the front of the steering head. This helps explain the curious frontal styling of the scooter that Michael Dregni described as having all the grace of a 'well-developed beer belly'!

DKR introduced two more scooters in 1958: the Pegasus with a 148cc Villiers 31C engine and three speeds and the Defiant with a 197cc Villiers 9E and four speeds. Then in 1959, the Manx completed the trio with a 249cc Villiers 2T twin-cylinder unit, four speeds and push-button starting.

At the end of 1959, the Dove II replaced the original with a 148cc 31C motor. The Pegasus II followed in 1960 with a 174cc 2L unit. Later

in 1960, these two models were axed in favour of the new Capella, which had a more shapely frontal styling job, and was to survive until DKR quit production in 1966.

## Triumph

Probably the most well known of all British motor cycle marques, and still going today under the direction of John Bloor, Triumph had its roots in the bicycle industry during Victorian times, being founded by a German immigrant, Siegfried Bettmann, in 1885. In 1902 Triumph built its first motor cycle.

After the Second World War, Triumph concentrated on their twins, whilst BSA, who by now owned Triumph, played around occasionally with the idea of producing a scooter (*see* earlier in this Chapter).

### Badge Engineering
The BSA Group employed a badge-engineering project that produced the BSA

Sunbeam and Triumph Tigress in mid-1958, both with a choice of either 175 single-cylinder two-stroke or 250 twin-cylinder four-stroke engines.

The two-stroke (based on the D7 Bantam and coded TS1) had bore and stroke dimensions of 61.5x58mm, giving a displacement of 172cc. However, many changes were made for its scooter application, whilst the gearbox owed much to the Triumph 200 Tiger Cub. Primary drive was by gears, the final drive by duplex chain. The front fork was a one-side affair with a single leg and twin tubes, one housing the spring, the other the damper. The frame comprised two tubes that ran parallel at the bolted-on steering head before angling out as they ran down and rearwards. After running under the engine and gearbox they turned upwards again and were joined at the top by a tube shaped to match the base of the dual seat. Both wheels were of 10in diameter with 3.50 section tyres.

The bodywork of the scooter was built up from pressed-steel panelling bolted together to form the front mudguard, apron, instrument panel, footboard and engine cover. The handle-bars also featured a small pressed-steel cover. A distinct disadvantage compared with the popular Italian scooters was that the body-work's main side sections were bolted together on the middle line, so routine maintenance was hindered by the two extremely small inspection panels.

As described elsewhere, the twin-cylinder Tigress was designated TW2 (6 volts, kick-starter) or TW2/S (12 volts, electric starting). However, both employed a 249cc parallel twin with engine dimensions of 56x50.6mm. Otherwise, the twin-cylinder models used identical running gear to the 175-engined machine.

Although afforded considerable publicity at their launch, the Triumph (and BSA) scooters did not prove very good sellers, but continued to be available, despite the general decline in

*The BSA Sunbeam scooter was offered in three versions – the B1 (175cc), B2 (250cc kick-start), and the B2S (250cc electric start). It was also badge-engined as the Triumph Tigress.*

scooter sales from 1960 onwards, until the mid-1960s.

**The Tina**
Even though the Tigress had hardly been a bestseller, Triumph entered the scooter market again in March 1962 with an all-new baby model, the Tina. As *Motor Cycle* reported, 'What was that? Just a little scooter, nothing to

*The Triumph range for 1959 from the American viewpoint, including its 175cc and 250cc Tigress scooter models, which were distributed by Johnson Motors and the Triumph Corporation.*

get excited about? You don't know Tina, that pert mam'selle from Meriden. Come and be introduced. No clutch lever, no gear pedal? That's right; just throttle and brakes – and an ingenious automatic transmission.'

Technically, the Tina (designed by Edward Turner) bristled with interesting features. For example, there was a box-section frame, through which air to the carburettor was drawn from a small grille just below the steering head. The front suspension by trailing-link was controlled by cylindrical rubber blocks in compression, whilst the engine, transmission and rear wheel pivoted as a single unit sprung by a single damper unit.

But the engine at least was of orthodox design, being a straightforward 99.75cc (50.4x50mm) single-cylinder two-stroke, the cylinder lying flat, with the head forward. Primary transmission was by a Goodyear-

*None other than racing car legend Stirling Moss with one of the twin-cylinder 250 Tigress models in London, circa 1958.*

made endless vee-belt running as pulleys, the diameters of which were varied according to engine load and road speed. In the rear hub there was a final reduction by helical gears. Overall ratios ranged from 5 to 14.75:1; the tyre sizes front and rear were 3.50x8.

Maximum speed was around 40mph (64km/h).

So far, so good. Unfortunately, on the day of its dealer launch, Edward Turner left for a six-month trip to the USA (not an uncommon event for him) and left Bert

*The overhead-valve parallel twin-cylinder power unit of the 250 Tigress (and BSA Sunbeam). It was powerful enough to give a maximum speed of 70mph (113km/h), which was exceptional for a scooter of the period.*

## The Triumph Tigress and BSA Sunbeam

Edward Turner might have been successful in his younger days with designs such as the Triumph Twin and Ariel Square Four. However, his scooter creations after the Second World War never reached such dizzy heights. Even the best – the Triumph Tigress TW2/TW2S and the badge-engineered BSA Sunbeam B2/B2S – were to prove commercial failures.

To begin with, by the time the Tigress and Sunbeam 250 twin-cylinder scooters appeared, it was too late – in fact ten years too late. Much of the problem was Turner himself. He stated at the launch of the new Triumph/BSA effort in late 1958, 'We are aiming at a specific chunk of this [scooter] market – let us say, the best half of the middle.' And he believed his own publicity. But actually, as events were to prove, he had totally misjudged the market, because scooter sales were about to begin a sudden steep decline.

This was unfortunate, because the Triumph/BSA scooter, at least the twin-cylinder version, was fast and economical, and offered potential scooter owners something different.

The purpose of using a 249.4cc (56x50.62mm) overhead-valve four-stroke twin-cylinder engine was to provide a level of performance superior to that usually associated with scooters. And in this Turner succeeded, so much so that the original prototype was so fast that it had to

be detuned for production! Even then the 250 Tigress/Sunbeam could easily exceed 70mph (113km/h) under favourable conditions.

For the technically minded, there was much to find of interest. The frame was an open duplex tubular structure looping out into a horizontal cradle that formed the basis for the flat floorboard and also carried the brackets in which the engine, gear unit and rear suspension were mounted. The front suspension, Vespa style, was supported by a massive steering head lug that was bolted to the frame. At the rear, swinging-arm suspension consisted of a cast-alloy casing for the fully enclosed final drive for the duplex chain. Primary drive was by gear from the engine mainshaft to the clutch centre, through a trio of clutch plates with bonded linings to the gearbox mainshaft, the latter running at half engine speed. The gear cluster was of constant mesh variety with an engagement mechanism of the type used on the Triumph Cub motor cycle. A neutral-finding device was incorporated, which by one stroke of a small pedal selected neutral from any gear except top.

As for the engine itself, the two vertical cylinders, crankcase and gearbox shell were cast as a single unit in aluminium alloy. The cylinder liners, of a special iron alloy, were cast in

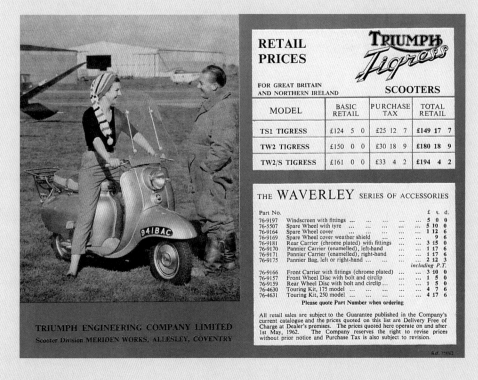

A 1962 Tigress price list of machines and accessories, the latter marketed under the Waverley brand name.

position. A manganese steel forging was used for the crankshaft which, having overlapping journals, possessed a high strength/weight ratio. It was mounted on a copper lead-alloy bearing on the timing side with a large, deep-groove ball-bearing in the drive side. Forged connecting rods of manganese steel alloy featuring steel-backed white metal liners for the big-end bearings. The pistons were of low-expansion silicon aluminium alloy.

The cylinder heads were formed in one unit of aluminium alloy with cast-in valve seat inserts of hard, heat-resisting material. Steel rockers and duralumin pushrods operated the overhead valves. Four cam lobes on a single shaft were driven by gears from the timing-side end of the crankshaft and, being set high, this allowed for short, stiff and light pushrods.

Wet-sump lubrication was employed, as on many cars, greatly simplifying much of the maintenance. On the timing side of the crankshaft, an external flywheel was mounted incorporating a turbine fan that delivered cooling air through ducting to the cylinder head and barrels. Also built into the flywheel was an AC generator rotor, the starter being bolted to the crankcase and cover. Two separate coils were used for the ignition, one for each cylinder. On the TW2/BS2 there was a 6-volt system, whereas the TW2S/BS2S electric start version was equipped with 12-volt electrics. Running on a compression ratio of 6.5:1, the engine generated 10bhp at 5,500rpm. Other details included a four-speed foot-operated gearbox, 10in wheels with 3.50 section tyres, a dry weight of 240lb (109kg) and a fuel tank capacity of 1.5 gal (6.5ltr).

*Extracts from the Tigress brochure, circa 1960 model year.*

When tested by *Motor Cycle Mechanics* in its March 1962 issue, tester Brian Smith had this to say about the model:

> The great flexibility of the machine was enhanced by the general comfort. There was very little noise from the engine and vibration only became distracting at high rpm ... I had only ridden the machine a couple of miles when I realized that here was a scooter which was definitely out of the ordinary. The steering, roadholding and general performance were equal to many motor cycles and better than most scooters.

However, there were also negative comments, such as a neutral selector which was 'not always reliable' and not only was the fuel tank too small, but the tap was under the seat, making life difficult.

And as there was no ignition key, just a switch, anyone could drive the machine away!

Production ended in 1965.

*The Triumph Tigress (and BSA Sunbeam) were built in three forms: 175, 250 and 250cc, with electric start.*

| Specification | 1958 BSA Sunbeam BS2/Triumph Tigress TW2 |
|---|---|
| Engine | Fan-cooled, overhead-valve, twin |
| Displacement | 249cc |
| Bore & stroke | 56x50.6mm |
| Gearbox | Four-speed, foot-change |
| Wheel size | 10in |
| Power | 10bhp |
| Maximum speed | 70mph (113km/h) |

now...you can **all** get about...

easy...easier...EASIEST! Yes, the TRIUMPH AUTOMATIC is, without doubt the easiest to handle of all vehicles, power or pedal, two wheels or four. It has two controls only — a twistgrip accelerator and brakes. If you've been accustomed to a clutch and gears you'll be amazed at the easy driving technique you get with the no clutch, no-gears Triumph Automatic — the all-purpose family vehicle.

TRIUMPH
AUTOMATIC T10

*Designed by Edward Turner (who also penned the Tigress 250), the Tina (a T10 version is shown) employed a simple transmission (vee-belt) with no gears or clutch.*

Hopwood to do the presentation. Subsequently, deliveries of the Tina were made to the dealer network, but unfortunately the factory was very soon afterwards forced to make many unscheduled collections to rectify faults that had befallen Triumph's baby scooter. Quite simply, the machines had been released before development had been fully completed. However, the bugs were eventually eradicated, and the Tina continued thereafter until mid-1965, when it was updated and rebadged as the T10, and in this form production ran until mid-1970.

## Sun

The Birmingham-based Sun Cycles & Fittings Co Ltd (Sun) originally manufactured bicycles, taking up motor cycle production in 1911. The company stopped producing motor cycles in 1932, but bicycle production continued. Post-war, powered two-wheelers appeared once more, headed in 1948 by a 98cc Villiers-engined auto cycle. Towards the end of 1956 Sun's first scooter was built. Again, this was powered by a 98cc Villiers unit.

Comprehensively shielded, the two-speed

machine called the Geni possessed several interesting features, not the least of which was that its Villiers 4F power unit was located well forward in the frame. Though there was a consequential loss of the flat floor favoured by most scooter designs, this did provide an improvement in weight distribution, this being further enhanced by the employment, unusual for a scooter, of large-diameter wheels shod with 2.50x17 tyres. A wire-mesh parcel basket was available as a cost option above the British price in October 1957 of £125.

But the real scooter from this brand came from mid-1959 onwards in the shape of the Sunwasp. The power unit was again a Villiers, but this time a 173cc (59x63.5mm) Mark 2L

of motor cycle pedigree, fitted out for scooter use with a fan on the nearside (left) of the crankshaft and with ducting to convey cooling air to the cylinder barrel and head. And since the Sunwasp was available in electric start form only, a Siba Dynastart unit was mounted on the offside (right) of the crankshaft end. In this system there was no separate starter motor, but when the starting button was pressed, current from the twin 6-volt batteries in series, giving a 12-volt system, would fire up the engine.

An unusual feature of the Sunwasp was its method of changing gear. On the offside of the floorboard were two pedals, set side-by-side, mounted on a common cross spindle and connected by rods to the three-speed gearbox

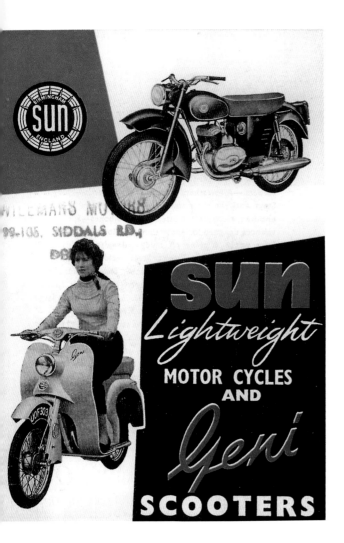

*Sun built not only lightweight motorcycles but scooters too, including the 98cc Villiers-powered Geni, which arrived in late 1956.*

in such a way that pressure on the left pedal produced downward changes, while upward changes were achieved by pushing the right pedal.

An advantage of the 12-volt electrical system was that not only was the horn surprisingly powerful, but the main beam of the headlamp gave an excellent spread of light, permitting daytime cruising speeds to be maintained after dark.

In spring 1958 Sun was acquired by Tube Investments (who already owned Norman and Phillips). As the 1960s dawned the new owners soon ceased scooter (and motor cycle) production, and Sun thereafter once again concentrated upon bicycle production.

## Excelsior

Excelsior, one of Great Britain's oldest motor cycle brands, began its commercial life as Bayliss, Thomas and Company in Coventry, the capital of the British cycle industry, the firm having built its first pedal cycle in 1870, transferring to motor cycles in 1896. Many well-known motor cycles were built during the inter-war years, by which time the company had relocated to Birmingham, most notably the legendary Manxman overhead-camshaft single. But after the Second World War it was all two-strokes, and except for the wartime Welbike (*see* earlier in this Chapter), Excelsior's entry into the scooter market did not begin until the spring of 1959, with the Monarch.

Actually the Mark I of this machine had a frame and bodywork from the DKR Dove scooter. There were two versions, one with an electric starter, designated EL, and the other with a kick-starter, the KS.

But a major difference was the power unit, the 147cc (55x62mm) assembly being manufactured by Excelsior themselves, featuring a built-up crankshaft supported by three journal ball-bearings, double-row rollers being employed for the big-end. A cast-alloy fan was used in the conventional crankshaft rotor position. Bolted to the rear of the engine was a three-speed Albion gearbox, controlled by heel-and-toe operation; both primary and final drives were by chain.

After testing out the scooter market with the Excelsior-powered, but DKR-framed and -bodied, Monarch Mark I for just over twelve

*A June 1960 brochure for the Excelsior Monarch Mark II scooter, powered by a 147cc Villiers engine with a three-speed foot-change gearbox.*

months, the company brought out a Mark II version with entirely new fibreglass bodywork designed by Fred White. A feature of this was that by simply freeing two wing nuts and disconnecting the rear light wiring, the entire body section could be lifted clear, thus providing unequalled accessibility to the mechanics of the machine.

The adoption of the fibreglass bodywork had also resulted in a considerable weight reduction – the Monarch Mark II, at 248lb (112.5kg), was over 50lb (23kg) lighter than its predecessor. As before, both electric start (weights quoted apply to this) and kick-start versions were offered.

## Panther

Although shown in prototype form on the Panther stand at the 1958 Earls Court Show in London, the production version of this scooter, the Princess, did not make its public bow until the end of 1959. The version sold to the public differed in a number of ways from the prototype. It had, for instance, a four-speed, instead of a three-speed gearbox and there were also modifications to the frame, transmission and wheel hubs. Externally, the most obvious change was to the bodywork, notably the rear panelling and the front mudguard. However, the basic frame design remained unchanged.

The power was provided by a fan-cooled 173cc Villiers 2L unit, which was available in both kick- and electric-start forms.

From the 1961 season it was also possible to order a 197cc version – again with either kick or electric start. The Princess continued to be produced until 1963, when its parent company, Phelon & Moore (P&M), went into receivership.

*Panther was an established motorcycle manufacturer that first branched out into the scooter world as the British importer for the French Terrot company in the mid-1950s. Later in that decade it introduced its own Princess model with a 173cc Villiers 2L unit. The machine shown dates from 1961 and has an electric start.*

## AMC

Associated Motor Cycles (AMC) originally came about as a result of various takeovers. The first was in 1931, at the height of the Great Depression, when Matchless, founded in 1899, acquired the equally famous and old-established AJS brand name. Next, in 1937, Matchless took over Sunbeam and later that year AMC was formed. Post-war acquisitions saw Francis-Barnett, James and finally Norton all swallowed up in 1947, 1950 and 1953 respectively.

During the remainder of the 1950s the AMC group did well, concentrating solely upon motor cycle production. Like the rest of the industry they had noticed the rise of scooter sales. But like many other motor cycle firms they did nothing for many years.

### The James

AMC only built one scooter model, the James 150, which was launched in the spring of 1960. Back in August 1959, an addition had been made to the range of two-stroke engines produced at AMC's Woolwich plant. This was viewed by outsiders as purely being for use in the Francis-Barnett and James range of light-weight motor cycles. But it did have a somewhat strange feature: the engine was bolted to its three-speed gearbox in such a way that the cylinder could be arranged vertically, with a forward inclination or horizontally. This last point was not picked up by either the press or public until news leaked out that AMC had a scooter under development, powered by a 150 engine, the cylinder of which lay horizontally under the floor.

However, the real reason for the choice of engine layout was two-fold. It gave a 45 front-wheel, 55 rear-wheel balance – the same as the James 250 Commodore motor cycle, thus offering the prospect of good handling. Secondly, the horizontal cylinder not only gave a low centre of gravity, but was, in the James design, exposed to the air stream by being located under the scooter's floorboards and so was amply cooled without the complications of fan and ducting.

The James 150 scooter displaced 149cc

(55x62.69mm) and both primary and final drives were by chain. The only major difference between the scooter's engine and that of the Flying Cadet motor cycle was that the cylinder was turned through ninety degrees, the carburettor (an Amal Monobloc) being on the right and the exhaust pipe on the left. Gear operation was by rocking pedal, whilst rear brake operation (by cable) was also by foot pedal.

In frame design the James broke away from conventional scooter practice, for the main member was a single tube formed into a hairpin loop. The loop edged the floor and weather shield, thus doubling up as a crash bar. The floor was comparatively flat and a large

inspection panel could be removed to provide access to the engine and transmission. A clever design feature was that by unlocking the dual seat it could be hinged open to reveal a large luggage compartment (big enough to store a helmet) and to its rear the fuel filler cap.

Front suspension was by pivoted fork, with a conventional, motor cycle-type swinging arm and twin shock absorber arrangement. With tyre sizes of 3.50x12 front and rear, the James was to prove one of the best-handling scooters.

There is no doubt that had this scooter appeared several years earlier it could well have proved a major sales success. As it was, it only

*A brochure for the James 150 scooter. Launched in the spring of 1960, its arrival sparked a major disagreement at senior management level within the controlling AMC group.*

ever sold in relatively small numbers. And the project was to cause a furious row between AMC Sales Director Jock West and the then Chairman of the group, Donald Heather. West was adamant that it wouldn't sell – and as events were to prove, it didn't – at least not in the required quantities. This disagreement triggered West's resignation from AMC in 1961.

In 1963, the James scooter, designated the SCI, was revamped with a four-speed gearbox (recoded SC4) and production ran through to AMC's demise in 1966.

*Some of the star features of the James design.*

## Raleigh

Raleigh of Nottingham was an old-established bicycle manufacturer, and pre-war had been closely involved with the motor cycle industry with its own range of machines and suppliers of the Sturmey Archer gearboxes. During the late 1950s it had begun building mopeds and in October 1960 it extended its interest in powered machines by announcing it had taken out a licence agreement with the Italian Bianchi concern to manufacture the 79cc *Orsetto* scooter (*see* Chapter 2). Raleigh's version was to be known as the Roma. Many have questioned why Raleigh didn't call it the

The star of the Scooter sphere.

Superbly styled for comfort and
offers de luxe, economy travel
horizontally mounted 3-speed
vigorous acceleration and a hi
exceptionally low fuel consump

The imaginative design of fram
bution of weight and low centr
stability and hair line steering
Scooter sphere.

The luxurious deep section foa
access to a spacious centre co
of safety helmets or parcels.
White and Devon Red/or Pea
a unique experience in conter

STAR F
1. Full width safety frame with robu
2. Expansive centre luggage compar
3. AC/DC Battery-Rectifier lighting
   beam swivelling headlamp and st
4. Deep built-in glove compartment
5. Pivoting fork, hydraulically damp
6. Unique, positive action toe and t
7. Even weight distribution and low
8. Starter pedal gearing and positio
   to ensure instant starting.
9. Light action, foot operated full v
   without effort.
10. High efficiency 149 cc. horizontal
    with an exceptionally smooth 3-s

A · JOY · TO · RIDE · AND

Milano, as Bianchi were based there. The answer is that the ISO Diva scooter was already being sold in Great Britain under that name.

## Ambassador

For many years the Ambassador firm of Berkshire were the British importers for the German range of Zündapp scooters and mopeds. However, they were also manufacturers in their own right, having begun motor cycle production back in 1946. Then, strangely, whilst still bringing in Zündapp Bella scooters, Ambassador launched its own scooter in October 1960. Actually, the newcomer looked remarkably like a Bella but it was powered by a British 173cc (59x63.5mm) Villiers Mark 3L fan-cooled, electric-start engine with a four-speed foot-change gearbox.

Ambassador was purchased by DMW in October 1962, when its founder and owner Kaye Don retired.

## Ariel

Ariel never made what could truly be called a scooter if one applies the formula of small-diameter wheels, comprehensive weather protection and footboards. However, two of its

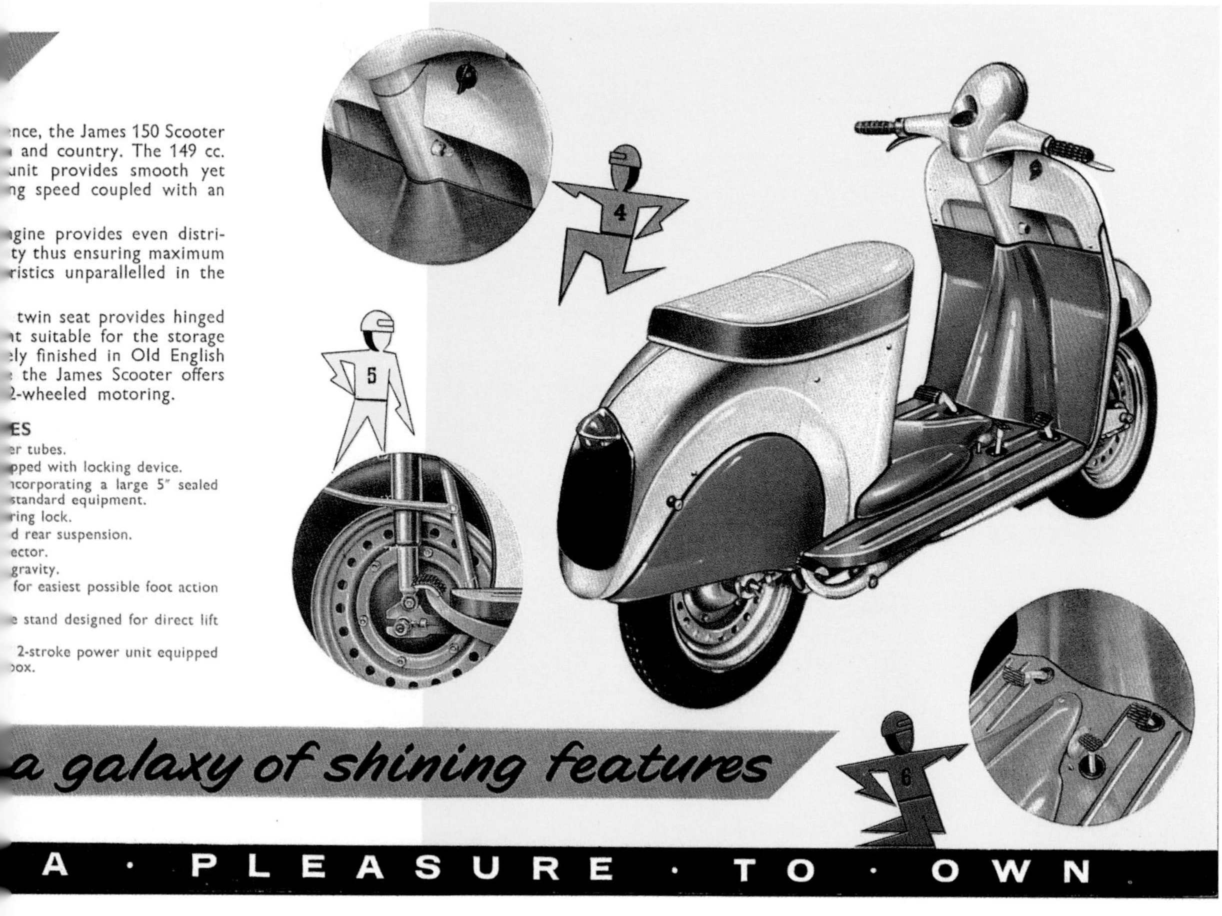

nce, the James 150 Scooter
and country. The 149 cc.
unit provides smooth yet
ng speed coupled with an

gine provides even distri-
ty thus ensuring maximum
ristics unparalleled in the

twin seat provides hinged
t suitable for the storage
ly finished in Old English
the James Scooter offers
2-wheeled motoring.

ES
r tubes.
pped with locking device.
ncorporating a large 5" sealed
standard equipment.
ring lock.
d rear suspension.
ector.
gravity.
for easiest possible foot action

stand designed for direct lift

2-stroke power unit equipped
ox.

*a galaxy of shining features*

A · PLEASURE · TO · OWN

# the revolutionary LEADER

*The Ariel Leader was a revolutionary design, combining the best parts of both scooter and motorcycle design; it was blessed by excellent performance and handling.*

products did meet with one or more of the above criteria.

The first was the Leader, designed by Val Page, which was launched in mid-1958. This was a genuine attempt at combining the best of motor cycle and scooter design in a single revolutionary package.

As I pointed out in my book *Ariel – The Complete Story* (Crowood, 2003):

> A part of the Leader's design was that it had been conceived very much as a whole, unified structure, not as a collection of components as was the case with more conventional machines. In many ways it was more akin to a grown-up scooter rather than a traditional naked motor cycle.

In many ways, the Leader was the ultimate high-performance (80mph/129km/h) large-capacity (247cc – 54x54mm twin-cylinder two-stroke engine) scooter-like machine of the classic era. But of course its lack of a U-shape frame and its large (16in) wheels rule it out as a true scooter.

*The Orsetto was built under licence in Great Britain by Raleigh Industries as the Roma – even though the Bianchi factory was in Milan!*

138

**FOR FAST SUMMER TOURING**

*in your holiday clothes —*

THE

**ARIEL**

*Leader*

**250 c.c. TWIN**

● *WHY EVEN CONSIDER whether you should choose a Scooter OR a Motorcycle, when you can have all the advantages of BOTH with the Leader. The cleanliness and weather protection of a Scooter plus fast touring at cruising speeds up to 65 m.p.h. Exhilarating acceleration with power to spare and the superb road holding qualities of the modern motorcycle at all speeds, under all conditions.*

**LDR 250**

**POST NOW** To: **ARIEL MOTORS LTD.,**
**SELLY OAK, BIRMINGHAM 29.**
Please send me illustrated literature and details of the Leader.

NAME

ADDRESS

M.C.I. 4.

*This 1958 launch advertisement reads: 'Why ever consider whether you choose a scooter or a motorcycle, when you can have both with the Leader.' But in the final reckoning, good as it was, it was shunned by scooter riders as being 'too motorcycle' and by motorcyclists as being 'too scooter'!*

In all, some 17,000 Leaders were manufactured over a seven-year period, ending in mid-1965. There was even a still-born 700cc flat-four four-stroke version, which never entered production.

The other Ariel model was the Pixie, a 49.94cc (38.9x42mm) overhead-valve with a four-speed, foot-change gearbox. The engine was the work of Edward Turner, whilst the chassis was taken care of by Val Page's successor at Ariel, Bernard Knight. The Pixie, best described as a scooterette-type machine, made its début at the Earls Court Show in November 1962, but did not go into production until some twelve months later. Like the 75cc BSA Beagle motor cycle, it was intended to be a British challenger to the Japanese, but both proved dismal sales failures, and although the Pixie continued to be available throughout 1964 and into 1965, few were sold. The whole exercise cost the BSA Group dearly.

## In Summary

As an observer at the 1960 London Show remarked:

> Reluctantly, painfully in a sense, Great Britain has inched her way deep into the scooter market. Long famous for powerful motor cycles, she couldn't believe at first that people really wanted these small-wheel, under-powered models on which you had to sit with no tank to tug between your knees – fancy, finicky, foreign machines with all the working parts hidden away behind expensive pressings.

Yes, that unfortunately was the widespread perception of the scooter world – and a very good reason why, for the most part, Great Britain was anything but great when it came to getting things done correctly as far as scooters were concerned. Although Great Britain, together with Italy and Germany, had by far the biggest number of manufacturers, its scooter production figures were way down on the other two.

At first, during the late 1940s and early 1950s, the British for the most part – we are of course talking about the manufacturing sector, not the customer – seemed to think it could ignore the tide of Vespas and Lambrettas.

But in the end, and much too late, the British industry had to face facts: people, the British public themselves, wanted to buy scooters; and the sight, year after year, of all those pounds, shillings and pence flooding away across the channel to continental Europe finally had its effect. Designers, draughtsmen, accountants – all went into action. The result was a diverse range of models produced by both newcomers and established motor cycle manufacturers, all trying to jump on the scooter bandwagon when it was already travelling along at high speed. The result was that many of these manufacturers got their fingers well and truly burned. One has a job trying to think of one really successful British scooter design in terms of sales. Even the mighty BSA Group got things terribly wrong. Others, like Velocette, borrowed large sums of money to fund scooter developments and came unstuck.

It is interesting to note that the two best-selling and longest-lived machines, the Velocette LE and the Ariel Leader were not, strictly speaking, scooters at all.

# 5 France, Belgium and Holland

## The French Scooter Industry

In general, the French were much quicker to design and market scooters than the British and a sizeable industry was ultimately created, with several major marques including Bernardet, Motobecane (Motoconfort), Peugeot and Terrot. However, the French rarely exported their products, and when they did it was in relatively small numbers, which meant that most French scooters remained within French borders.

As in Great Britain and West Germany, the Italian scooter giant Piaggio had concluded a licence agreement early on, which meant that Vespas were constructed in France by *Ateliers de Construction de Motocycles et d'Accessories* (ACMA) from 1950. Actually, the first 1,200 examples were imports. By 1951, a total of just under 9,000 Vespas were partially built in France. However, by 1952, 28,280 were built by ACMA, totally of French construction. Manufacturing continued apace until 1962, when ACMA was forced to cease production due to the financial weakness of the French economy.

Following ACMA's success with the Vespa, another French company, *Société Industrielle de Troyes* (SIT) reached a similar licence agreement with Piaggio's rivals, Innocenti, to manufacture Lambrettas in France.

## Bernardet

The three Bernardet brothers had begun building cars and sidecars at a factory in Bourg-la-Reine during the immediate aftermath of the Second World War, but soon added scooters to their portfolio.

Their first model had the designation of A.48. This was powered by a 128cc Ydral two-stroke engine, with its four-speed gearbox located next to the rear wheel of the machine. This pioneering French scooter was comprehensively enclosed and on its large weather shield was the badge of the Bernardet-Frères coat of arms that was also to be found on future Bernardet scooters.

The next model, the A.49, was essentially an updated version of the original, retaining the 4.00x12 tyre size of the A.48, but with improved cooling and more refinement.

When the *Salon de Paris* Show opened in October 1949, the Bernardet brothers presented a much more ambitious scooter, the B.250. This was powered by a 249cc Violet split-single two-stroke power unit designed by the well-known French engineer Marcel Violet. The bodywork remained much as before, although benefiting for the first time from rear suspension. The power unit produced a claimed 10bhp.

During 1950, both the 125 and 250 Series machines were revamped, as the C.50 with the 125cc Ydral engine, and as the BM using a development of the Violet unit.

Next, at the 1951 *Salon de Paris*, Bernadet displayed a prototype coded E.51. This employed a new 125cc engine, designed and built by Bernardet themselves. With smaller diameter 8in wheels and a superior power-to-weight ratio, the newcomer produced 6bhp

*The Bernadet B series 250 scooter made its début at the Salon de Paris in October 1949, the BM250 (seen here) arriving in 1950. The styling is typical of the company's scooters.*

[which débuted, appropriately, in 1952]. The cowhand's scooter came complete with rhinestone saddlebags, fringed handlebars, and studded seats with a saddlehorn on the rear pillion. Displayed at the *Salon de Paris* on a rug of simulated white cowhide, the only thing missing was cowhorns on the front fender.

In 1955, the Bernardet operation was acquired by the Le Poulain Company, which led to the use of its Servomatic transmission system on Bernardet models. This coincided with the introduction of smaller-engined models, which were devoid of the earlier distinctive style that had made the Bernardet scooters stand out from the crowd. These newcomers were at first powered by a 49cc engine, but were later increased in size to 85cc and designated the Cabri L6 and M60. The Cabri line was also marketed in Belgium as the *Hirondelle Passe-Partout* (all-purpose swallow).

Another machine, which was first seen in 1955, was the *Guépar* (Cheetah). Equipped with a twin-cylinder engine, this had at first been called the Jaguar, but was changed after legal communication from the British car firm of the same name.

Bernadet scooters lived on until 1959, but never recaptured the spirit or sales of the earlier models.

## Terrot

Charles Terrot was one of the French motoring pioneers, having constructed tricycles and quads during the late 19th century, prior to building his first motor cycle in 1902. During the 1930s Terrot was famous for its range of unit construction engines.

Samuel Renaud presented the first Terrot scooter, the VMS, at the *Salon de Paris* in October 1951. Powered by a 2.6bhp 98cc engine with a two-speed gearbox, it was notable for its bulbous bodywork, which was reminiscent of period American car design.

and had a four-speed gearbox. Also, there was now an offside (right) mounted kick-starter, which replaced the awkward to use rearside (left) of the Ydral-powered machines.

Bernadet's top of the range 250 model was redesignated the D.51 and, according to the company, could reach 56mph (90km/h). Of all the Bernardet machines, the 250-engined models were ultimately to prove the most popular and long-lasting.

Another version was what Michael Dregni described as:

The stereotype of the American cowboy come to life in the coveted 'Texas' version of the Y.52

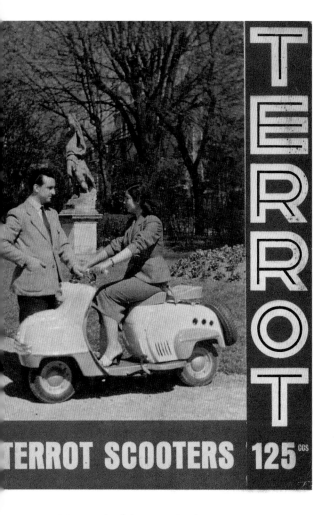

*Terrot produced the VMS3 that featured a three-speed pre-selective gearbox and was imported into the UK by Phelon & Moore (Panther).*

When placed into production it normally sported a two-tone paint finish and had both front and rear suspension systems fully enclosed. The wheels were 8in with 3.50 section tyres.

It was revised and redesignated the VMS2 for the 1953 season with an increase in engine size to 124cc (53.5x55mm) and a power output of 3.5bhp, but it still retained a two-speed gearbox.

Finally, in 1954, came the VMS3 with a three-speed pre-selector gearbox. Sold from

1955 in Great Britain by P&M Panther as the Scooterot, the VMS3's pre-selection was achieved by rotation of the nearside (left) twist-grip. A small window in the cast-alloy handlebar clamp framed a visual gear-position indicator. After pre-selection of the required gear, operation of the left pedal effected engagement. A conventional clutch control was used when moving off from rest.

On both the VMS2 and VMS3, which besides their gearboxes were otherwise identical, fan-cooling was employed for the two-stroke single-cylinder units. Primary drive was by gears and the final drive chain featured a pressed-steel cover. A knob protruding through the front of the engine cowling brought into operation the carburettor choke, which was automatically released as soon as the throttle was opened.

A tubular, duplex-loop frame carried a bolted-on sub-frame. Mounted on stub axles, Vespa-fashion, the wheels were interchangeable.

From 1953 until their demise in 1958, Magnat-Debon (founded by Joseph Magnat and Louis Debon in 1893) built the Terrot scooters in a badge-engineering exercise as the 98cc SI (VMS), the S25 and the S3 with larger 124cc engine units, the latter with a pre-selector gearbox.

Terrot, which had been owned by Peugeot since 1954, ceased production in 1961.

## Motobecane/Motoconfort

Founded by Abel Bardin and Charles Benóit, the company built its first motor cycle in 1922 and soon became one of the French industry's largest producers. The first major model of the post-war era was the bestselling 50cc Mobylette moped.

Motobecane (sometimes sold under the Motoconfort banner), entered the scooter arena in October 1951 at the Paris Show, with a 125cc four-stroke model, designed by Géo

*Magnat-Debon badge-engineered the Terrot scooter as the Type S3 and Type S25.*

Ham. With 8in wheels, this produced 5bhp at 5,000rpm and was sold as the Motobecane SCC and Motoconfort STC.

Next came the SB (Motobecane) and SV (Motoconfort). One of the SB's was displayed at the Earls Court Show, London in November 1954. The new 124cc (54x54mm) two-stroke engine formed a single unit with a three-speed gearbox and cast-aluminium oil bath which enclosed the final drive chain and also carried the rear wheel stub axle. The complete engine-transmission unit pivoted on the frame, which comprised a single, large-diameter tube. Notably, the suspension medium, both front and rear, was rubber; at the front by rubber bands! The wheel size had also been increased to 10in in diameter.

The styling is best described as being a French take on the Lambretta D.

Next, at the end of 1955, came the SVH/SBH. Essentially these were de luxe versions of the SV/SB models. Now the engine was completely enclosed, with only the wheels left naked. An interesting technical feature was that an aluminium cylinder was now used on the two-stroke engine – unlinered, but with the bore hard chromium-plated.

Next, in 1958, the engine of the two-stroke was enlarged to 144cc (59x54mm). It was simply a larger-bore version of the old unit, so it was still fan-cooled, with chromium-plated bore and three speeds.

The import of the Motobecane scooter was handled in Great Britain by Motor Imports (a division of dealers Pride & Clarke) of London. A pillion seat and spare wheel were included on British imports as standard equipment, where it was marketed as the Mobyscooter.

## Peugeot

Not only can Peugeot claim to be the second oldest surviving automobile manufacturer, but also one of the oldest two-wheeled marques. The first Peugeot 'car' arrived in 1888 but was in fact a steam-powered three-wheeler! The Peugeot motor cycle made its début in 1899.

As today, the two-wheeled arm of the Peugeot empire trades as Cycles Peugeot and is a separate division from its more well-known four-wheeled brother.

Right from its launch in 1953, the Peugeot scooter adopted a formula of a 125/150cc engine and three-speed gearbox atop 8in wheels with a flat floor layout due to its duplex frame.

Only the largest-engined version was ever officially imported into Great Britain, by Christie & Slater of London, deliveries beginning in 1956.

The 147cc (56x60mm) single-cylinder two-stroke engine was fan-cooled with unit construction of the gearbox, control of the latter being of the twist-grip type. The final drive chain was enclosed within a cast-aluminium case which formed the pivoted arm of the rear suspension.

The front wheel was carried on a trailing arm and both wheels were sprung on the Neiman rubber-band system which, Peugeot claimed, was sufficiently progressive to eliminate the need for separate dampers. Access to the spark plug and fuel filler was gained by raising the rider's saddle, but for major maintenance the complete main body section could be hinged forward, exposing the engine and transmission.

Stowage for luggage and oddments had received more than average attention. Below

The 150 c.c. Moby Scooter has everything that the most fastidious and exacting enthusiast desires. Beautifully styled and designed to give maximum rider comfort, it has a performance and economy which must be experienced to be believed. Never was the French genius for combining good looks with practical efficiency more exemplified than by the Moby Scooter. Acclaimed by the experts it is undoubtedly the best 150 c.c. Scooter buy to-day!

**Moby scooter**

**150 c.c.**

**£149.17.7 (inc. P.T.)**

**Engine:** Two stroke double transfer single cylinder, fan cooled, special cast iron lined aluminium cylinder. Capacity 150 c.c.

**Transmission:** Gear primary drive to gearbox; rear by roller chain fully enclosed.

**Gearbox:** Three-speed with multiplate clutch controlled by left-hand handlebar lever and twist grip.

**Ignition:** Flywheel magneto, high tension, with automatic advance.

**Chassis:** Single girder frame of electro-welded steel tubing with full front cowl giving full protection.

**Mudguards:** Heavy dome section affording adequate weather protection at all times.

**Suspension:** Front: Link with patented Neiman Rubber Rings. Rear: Swinging Arm with Evigdon Hutchinson Rubber Cushioning.

**Wheels:** Interchangeable, with balloon 3.5 × 10 tyres.

**Brakes:** Internal expanding hub brakes. Rear controlled by foot pedal; front by handlebar lever.

**Electrical Equipment:** 6-volt headlamp with dipping switch, rear lamp and horn.

**Speedometer:** Built into headlamp.

**Finish:** Attractively enamelled in cream/maroon. All bright parts chromium plated.

**Equipment:** Pillion seat, spare wheel. Comprehensive tool kit in large heavy duty steel container.

**Optional Extras:** Rear luggage carrier, chromium plated, £5. Front luggage carrier, stove enamelled, £2.5.0.

**Weight:** 216 lbs.

**Speed:** Approximately 45/50 m.p.h.

**Fuel Consumption:** Approximately 80/90 m.p.g.

*Arriving in 1958 and sold in the UK by Motor Imports as the Mobyscooter, the Motobecane SBH used a 144cc (59×54mm) fan-cooled two-stroke engine with a chrome-plated cylinder bore.*

the instrument panel was a lockable glove compartment and the almost flat top of the mudguard nose opened to reveal a further compartment of a useful capacity. The lid was equipped with slats to accommodate suitcases or other bulky articles. Standard equipment included twin-sprung saddles, a steering lock and a spare wheel, the centre of which housed the rear number plate.

There were a number of improvements for the 1958 season (the model now being coded SI5B in Great Britain). The most obvious was the transfer of the headlamp from a position on the windshield to a neat handlebar location (so that the light now turned with the 'bars'). New too was a quickly detachable panel below the dashboard to provide easier access to the control cables.

A year later, towards the end of 1958, the SI5C made its bow. The most noticeable difference between the new C and outgoing B was that the front luggage locker was dispensed with, its place being taken by a neatly styled mudguard, which moved with the wheel, and a cowling incorporating the horn around the base of the steering head. Another change was that the C employed 10in instead of 8in wheels, thus giving improved ground clearance.

British imports were now handled by Scooter Concessionaires of London.

Peugeot scooters were also marketed under the Griffon/FMC brand – more badge engineering.

Production of all types ceased at the end of the 1950s.

## Monet–Goyen and Manurhin

Of the remaining French scooter manufacturers, the two most notable were Monet–Goyen and Manurhin – for totally different reasons.

The former had been a pioneer in the very early days of scooter-like machines, having built their Vélauto back in 1919 and later the

*A brochure, dated September 1954, for Peugeot's 125 S.55. Note the front mudguard with integral parcel grid, sprung saddles and suspension on both wheels.*

Super Vélauto, powered by British Villiers 147 and 270cc two-stroke engines.

Monet-Goyen had built its Villiers engines in France under licence from the mid-1930s. They returned to the scooter world in 1953 with the Starlett – again using Villiers power – in the shape of a 98cc unit and featuring full enclosure. Developments of the original Starlett were continued throughout the remainder of the 1950s, together with a range

of lightweight motor cycles. However, all Monet-Goyen production ceased in 1959.

The Manurhin was formerly known as the DKW Hobby (*see* Chapter 3) and when the German firm ceased production of this model, the rights were purchased in 1957 by the French concern and they manufactured it under their own name, incorporating minor changes. As with the German original, its most interesting feature was the Uher Beltomatic system of variable transmission, which provided the equivalent of two-pedal control in a car. Power from the 74cc two-stroke engine fed to a self-engaging clutch and then by belt as expanding and contracting pulleys. On the move, the engine speed was automatically related to load and road speed. Wheels were large by scooter standards, the tyre size being 2.75x16 front and rear.

## Other French Manufacturers

Other French scooter marques during the period covered by this book included: Ardent, Cazenave, Lefol, Martin-Moulet, Mars, OLD, PP Roussey, Paul Vallée, Ravat, Scootavia and Sterling, but the lion's share of the production went to the largest companies as detailed earlier.

## Belgium

In comparison to the French, Belgian scooter production was small, with only a handful of companies. There were six Belgian producers: Aldimi, Buydens, Claeys-Flandria, Lenobile, Minerva-Van Hauwaert and Saroléa.

## Aldimi

Aldimi, based in the capital Brussels, began in 1953 with the royally named Prince de Liège scooter, using a bought-in Saroléa 124cc engine that produced 6bhp at 4,800rpm, with

10in wheels and 3.50 section tyres. In 1954 a 197cc Saroléa-engined version was offered. However, sales not were particularly successful for either version. So in 1956 Aldimi began building the Piatti scooter, this of course being far better known in Great Britain (*see* Chapter 4).

## Claeys-Flandria

Based in Zedelgem, Claeys-Flandria launched its first scooter in 1954, powered by a German Ilo engine with a displacement of 174cc. Then in 1956 it concluded a licence agreement to build the Italian SIM *Ariete* (ram) with a 149cc (57x58mm) engine, its most interesting feature being its shaft final drive via a single-sided swinging arm manufactured in aluminium. The final Claeys-Flandria scooter was its 1960

49cc Parisienne two-stroke with a four-speed gearbox.

## Lenobile

Lenobile, with production facilities in Brussels and Charleroi, built its first scooter, the Kon-Tiki in 1952. Michael Dregni described it as 'the scooter with the oddest name and silliest bodywork' and styling which, 'looked like a coffin on wheels with a headlamp and wind-shield on top'. The Kon-Tiki and all subsequent Lenobile scooters were powered by German Sachs engines.

## Minerva

Minerva was founded by Sylvain de Jong to produce bicycles towards the end of the 19th

*The Manurhin was formerly known as the DKW Hobby. When the German firm ceased production, the rights were purchased by the French concern.*

Scooter
MANURHIN

*The only Scooter in the World with an entirely automatic transmission*

**Simplicity in starting.
Simplicity in driving.**
Thanks to this remarkable feature, the Manurhin scooter is controlled as easily and simply as a modern automobile with an automatic transmission.
The three horse-power motor can easily handle two people on any road — on the level, or in the mountains. The "Variator" always selects the proper ratio between motor and rear wheel speed to give maximum performance under changing conditions.
The speed (limited purposely to 40 m.p.h.) coupled with the 16 in. wheels, the front telescopic fork and rear swinging arm suspension, combine to give this machine the comfort, safety, stability and ease of operation, which every one has been seeking.
The price is within reach of every one.
The MANURHIN is not only an evolution, it is a REVOLUTION.

century, beginning motor cycle production in 1900 and so was a true pioneer of the Belgian two-wheeled industry. However, it did not produce motor cycles after 1909, concentrating on cars up to 1939.

Then in the early 1950s, the old Antwerp firm was sold to Van Hauwaert of Brussels and the Minerva name returned to two wheels in 1953 with a 150cc scooter that was in fact an Italian MV Agusta built under licence. At the Brussels show that year, the company displayed a prototype tricar, using two of the scooters at the front and a single rear wheel. Then in 1954, the company introduced its Motoretta scooter powered by a German Ilo two-stroke engine, displacing 173cc.

## Saroléa

Like Minerva, Saroléa was a famous old motor cycle manufacturer, having built its first example in 1898, but unlike Minerva it had continued two-wheeled production. However, by the mid-1950s it was finding the going tough and in 1956 Saroléa joined the ranks of the scooter manufacturers with the launch of its *Dijnn* (goblin) machine at the Brussels Show. But in reality the *Dijnn* was just a re-badged Italian Rumi *Formichino*. Saroléa then built quantities of the Rumi design under licence for the Belgian market, until Rumi themselves ceased production of scooters in the early 1960s.

## Holland

Like Belgium, scooter production in Holland was small with only a few companies.

## Bitri

The Bitri range of scooters was manufactured by the Dokkum-based *Nederlandse Scooterfabrik*

(NV) concern, and was produced from 1954 until the early 1960s.

The Bitri was first displayed in 1954, and was powered by a German Ilo 118cc two-stroke engine, producing 4.5bhp at 4,500rpm through a two-speed gearbox. In 1955, this was joined by a 143cc Ilo-engined machine. Then in 1957, a new, more powerful Bitri arrived with a 191cc Sachs power unit, producing 10.2bhp at 5,250rpm. By 1960 the Bitri range comprised four scooters: the 150-4 KS standard and Luxe, the 150-4 ES and the 200-4 ES; (KS denoting kick-start and ES electric start).

## Eysink

Eysink, as a powered two-wheeler manufacturer, was in existence for some seventy-five years, from 1899 until the late 1970s. D. H. Eysink, who founded the company, had become interested in motor cycles and automobiles at the turn of the 20th century. Thereafter Eysink built a wide range of motor cycles for both street and racing use. In fact Eysink was the only Dutch manufacturer to compete before and after the Second World War in road racing. In 1948, the new 125cc class was introduced at the annual Dutch TT, and the local Eysink machines emerged victorious.

From the early 1950s, Eysink produced scooters with 98 and 249cc engine sizes. But from the late 1950s it concentrated mainly on 50cc ultra-lightweight scooterettes and motor cycles, plus mopeds.

## Wabo

The third and final Dutch scooter brand was Wabo, which built scooters during the 1950s powered exclusively by British Villiers engines – the 98cc 4F with a two-speed gearbox and the 147cc 30C with three speeds.

# 6 The USA

## New and Old

The American Autoped (and Motoped) of 1915–16 is viewed as the world's first real scooter (*see* Chapter 1). The USA had a surprisingly high number of scooter manufacturers over the years, many of these being in business long before Piaggio and Vespa came along to launch the modern machine. Pre-1945 US scooter names included Bangor Scootmaster, Comet, Crocker, Cushman, Custer, Le Jay, Le Ray, Mead-Cycle, Moto Glide, Moto-Scoot, Mustang, Powell, Rock-Ola, Safeticycles, Salsbury, Sportcycle and Trotwood.

However, only a few of these names returned to scooter manufacture following the end of the Second World War. During the late 1940s, American scooter manufacturers consisted of the remaining pre-war ones: Cushman, Mead-Cycle, Moto-Scoot, Mustang, Powell, Rock-Ola and Salsbury, plus a batch of newcomers: Beam, Clark Engineering, Globe, Lowther Ronnay (Ronard) and Speedway. But the vast majority of the latter names soon faded from the scene.

## Rock-Ola

Rock-Ola is an excellent example of an American scooter producer in the early 1930s. A Canadian citizen, David C. Rockola launched into business in Chicago during the early 1930s, initially building weighing machines. Then, in 1935, Rockola – trading under the Rock-Ola brand name – designed and built his first jukebox, which proved the making of the man.

In 1938, Rock-Ola entered the scooter world with a typical small-wheeled, minimalist, 1930s American design as originally laid down by Salsbury. A Rock-Ola advertisement of 1938 read:

America's Newest Mode of Transportation – Rock-Ola Motor Scooter. Go places, quickly, inexpensively! … It's loads of fun to go 'Scooting'! And you can easily learn to ride in one minute. Grand for going to and from work, school or shopping. Convenient to use – and parks anywhere. Safe, comfortable, and featuring the revolutionary new 'Floating Ride'!

The 'floating ride' referred to the scooter's front suspension, via triangulated forks and dual coil springs.

Rock-Ola also offered a three-wheeled delivery truck version with two wheels and a goods container at the front, and the engine in the scooter's rear section.

Post-war, Rock-Ola concentrated upon jukeboxes, leaving scooters to others.

## Cushman

Of all the many and varied American scooter manufacturers, the Cushman brand was both the longest lived and most well known in the USA.

The Cushman Motor Works had been founded by cousins Clinton and Everett Cushman, who had begun building two-stroke engines for power boats in their basement during 1901. They had been issued with their first patent in 1902 (for a two-stroke engine), this being used to power anything from washing machines to separators. Soon the Cushmans used this expertise in engine design to build two-stroke marine racing units. A purpose-built factory was constructed in 1913, where their famous Husky powerplant, an air-cooled single-cylinder four-stroke, was produced in 1922.

Cushman's first scooter, the Auto-Glide, was inspired by E. Foster Salsbury's Motor Glide. And it came about like this: Salsbury had contacted Cushman in the summer of 1936, regarding the purchase of 1,000 Husky engine units to power a development of his Motor Glide. Later, when Salsbury passed up Cushman's offer regarding the engines, he decided to use them himself on what was to emerge as the Auto-Glide.

As Cushman's former president Robert H. Ammon told Michael Dregni during a 1992 interview, 'We were in the business of selling engines. The idea of making a motor scooter was to build and sell more engines.'

## The Great Depression

As for most American firms, the Great Depression following the Wall Street Crash of October 1929 was not kind to Cushman. In 1934, John F. Ammon and his son Charles took over Cushman. The family line was carried on through Charles Ammon's son, Robert H. Ammon.

During the late 1930s, the Auto-Glide model was built and sold in an amazing array of designations. The first truly post-war models, the 52, 52A and 54 were produced during the period 1946–48 and the Auto-Glide name was axed. Thereafter, all the scooters were known as Cushmans. But although the name had changed, the boxy styling and mechanical components remained largely the same.

Then, during late 1948, Cushman introduced its new model named the Variamatic with a belt-drive torque-converter, automatic transmission and clutch, and added the B designation to the 54 model coding. However, the Variamatic proved unreliable in service and was soon dropped.

## The 60, 711 and 720 Series

In 1949, the 62 Pacemaker, the first of the new 60 series, was produced. Later scooters in this series included the 62A Sport, 64 Road King and 61 Highlander. Next came the 711 Highlander (1950–58), and developments of the series including the 714 (1952–53) and 715 (1953–58).

However, it was the 720 series that transported Cushman into the modern scooter age. As Michael Dregni commented, 'It was a modernistic vision of the scooter of the future with fibreglass bodywork and Jet Age styling.'

But the 720 series (including the 721, 722 and 725) never really caught on – and by 1961 the series was no more and Cushman was importing Vespas from Italy. But this too was not a success, with only some 5,000 units being sold in three years.

## The Eagle Series

At the same time as Cushman launched its 60 series in 1949, it also introduced a totally different scooter – the Eagle – which is best described as a scooter that looked as if it had been bred with a Harley-Davidson or an Indian v-twin! As Robert H. Ammon recalled later, 'Somebody in our sales department wanted a scooter that looked like a motor cycle with a gas tank between your legs. It turned out to be a hell of a good idea.' The Eagle looked like a motor cycle in miniature – and it certainly did not follow standard scooter practice, even though it did have small diameter wheels. However, except for its small wheels and low build, can the Eagle series (which ran until the mid-1960s) really be counted as a scooter? This is a good question and in truth there are many others, such as the British Velocette LE and the Italian Moto Guzzi *Gallatto,* that are equally hard to define, to say nothing of certain other American 'scooters'.

But what is not in doubt is that the Cushman Eagle proved popular and its production life, in various model codes, was long, spanning 1949–64.

### The Trailster

Débuting in 1960, the Trailster (coded 723) was another Cushman oddball, but this time it was half motor scooter, half jeep. Based on the running-gear (frame and front forks) of the 720 series, the Trailster employed a two-speed, sliding-gear transmission. Largely intended for off-road use, Cushman also provided an optional (higher gear) sprocket set for tarmac use. Unusual features of the Trailster also included a 'tractor tread' rear tyre, a 'game & gear' luggage carrier and *two* foot brake pedals – one on either side!

### Cushman's Demise

For the first decade of the post-war era, Cushman took the lion's share of the American scooter market. However, during the latter half of the 1950s, things began to change, some of this due to more competition from both inside and outside the country. In addition, government legislation with tougher traffic laws for young riders (their main market) saw Cushman's fortunes fall, and in early 1965 production of the Eagle ceased.

## Powell

Based in Los Angeles, the brothers Channing and Hayward Powell built their first scooter, the Streamliner Series 40, in 1939. This followed the set-in-stone formula first used by Salsbury in the mid-1930s of step-through frame, rear-mounted engine, automatic clutch and small wheels. Power came from a Lauson four-stroke single-cylinder engine, which Powell's sales brochure called 'forced blast cooling' – in other words – by fan!

Another Powell sales blurb centred around the Centri-Matic automatic clutch, which was in fact a centrifugal clutch with only one speed. Final drive was via chain to the rear wheel, the sprocket for the latter being integral with the hub. A definite advantage of the Streamliner was that it featured both front and rear suspension.

In 1941, the Series 40 was replaced by the 41-J. This was still referred to as the Streamliner, its main difference being the use of an engine-driven generator to provide lighting power, rather than the earlier model's magneto.

In 1940, the Powell operation moved to a new production facility in California. To celebrate this event they introduced an entirely new model: the A-V-8 (Aviate), which was very much a motor cycle in miniature in the style of the Mustang (*see* page 152) and the Cushman Eagle mentioned previously. Its four-stroke engine made a point of using components such as connecting rods, valves, springs, guides and the like from the Ford V8 car. Although a kick-starter was standard, for what is claimed as a first in the scooter world, an electric starter was a cost option. Tyre size was 8in.

At first, the A-V-8 employed a variable-speed V-belt system similar to that used earlier by Salsbury. The centrifugal clutch drove a variable-speed transmission via a rubber V-belt, which could be moved manually into any one of four speeds, plus a fifth-speed overdrive, final drive being by chain. But in service this transmission did not prove a success.

It should be mentioned that when Powell switched from peacetime production to government war contracts at the end of 1942, versions of the A-V-8 were marketed by the Cooper, Clark and Ronney (Ronard) firms.

**Post-War**

Following the end of the conflict, Powell returned to scooters via the new Lynx economy model, powered by a Wisconsin AKN unit giving around 6bhp, with magneto ignition, automatic clutch and 4.00x7 tyres.

Next came the C47 of 1947, which made a return to an in-house Powell powerplant and developments of this design continued until 1951.

In 1949, Powell made a return to its mini-motor cycle theme with the P-81, which was built until 1951. With a 392cc engine, together with a dry weight of 190lb (86kg), the newcomer could cruise all day at 45mph (72km/h). And with more power and larger 12in wheels, the P-81 was in many ways superior to Cushman's very similar Eagle that made its début around the same time.

During the Korean War Powell once again quit scooter production for war contracts. And although the company did make a return (the last Powell scooter being built in 1972), the brothers had quickly moved into the four-wheeled market, in the shape of pick-up trucks and camper vans.

**Mustang**

Mustang (named after the famous American wartime P-51 Mustang fighter aircraft) entered production in late 1945 with its Colt mini-motor cycle. The first machines were powered by the British Villiers 122cc (50x62mm) two-stroke 9D engine. However, throughout 1946 and into 1947, supplies of the Villiers unit were extremely difficult to obtain.

Mustang was owned by Gladdon Products of California, a large engineering concern that during the immediate post-war period had been taken over the Kinner Motor Co., the latter firm having built a five-cylinder radial engine for the US Army Air Corps. But before Kinner hit financial trouble it had switched to producing a 317.6cc side-valve single-cylinder engine for industrial use. Nicknamed the 'Bumble Bee', this had originally been used in the war to power airborne generator units.

With modifications, the Bumble Bee replaced the Villiers as the motive power for the Mustang two-wheeler. And so the Colt became the Model 2 (built from 1947 through

*Together with the Cushman Eagle and the Powell A-V-8 (Aviate), the Mustang series were as much mini-motorcycles as scooters.*

*The Mustang was named after the famous American wartime P-51 fighter aircraft.*

to 1950). However, British components were still in evidence in the shape of an Amal carburettor and Burman foot-change four-speed gearbox. And in 1947, the Mustang had become the first American-powered two-wheeler to use telescopic front forks.

By the end of the 1940s Gladdon had placed the Mustang operation in its own separate division, with Howard Forrest and Chuck Gardner as chief engineer and production manager respectively, these two having built the first prototype of what was to emerge as the Mustang Colt back in 1944.

During the 1950s Mustang models were defined as the 3, 4 (a 'delivery' cycle), 5 and the like. But conversely, it also employed the Colt name (on the Model 4 de Luxe of 1956–58). Then came the Pony (1959–65), the Bronco (1959–65), the Stallion (1959–65) and the Thoroughbred (1960–65). Another version, intended to cash in on the growing off-road boom that was sweeping the USA during the 1960s, was the Trail Machine (1962–65).

Strangely, just as the Villiers engine supplies had stunted Mustang's early production plans, it was another British supplier, Burman, who

was to cause its ultimate demise in 1966. With the many British motor cycle manufacturers transferring to unit-construction engines, and the AMC group (AJS, Matchless and Norton) now using their own gearboxes, Burman was forced to quit the market. This left Mustang without a supplier of this vital part. And this, together with the rise of the Japanese, spelled its end.

In American terms the Mustang was a considerable scooter success, but was it truly a scooter? Like the Cushman Eagle it was in reality more of a miniature motor cycle than a conventional scooter.

## Allstate

Allstate was the brand name for a series of scooters (and motor cycles) marketed by mail-order specialists Sears, Roebuck & Co. via its catalogue, all over the USA from the end of the Second World War to the early 1960s.

The first scooters marketed by the organization came in 1950 via Cushman, soon followed by Vespa in 1951. Both these were little more than a re-badging exercise, with the original Cushman or Vespa logo replaced on the windshield by the Allstate name. Over the years various model names were used from simply 'Standard' or 'de Luxe', to Jetsweep. Sears had also begun selling Puch motor cycles from 1954 and the Compact scooter during the early 1960s; this was actually a 60cc Puch Cheetah (*see* Chapter 3).

In 1961, Sears and Cushman had a fall-out, Sears choosing to concentrate upon its Vespa and Puch lines, whilst Cushman responded by axing its own scooter range, and instead also imported Vespas from Italy! This set of events did not help either Sears or Cushman, because the former dropped all scooters from its catalogue from 1963, whilst Cushman themselves were gone by the mid-1960s.

## Harley-Davidson

Harley-Davidson might have been number one for motor cycle production in the USA, but it was a latecomer to the scooter world and of course it was – for many – hard to associate Harley-Davidson, makers of the legendary V-twin motor cycle, with a scooter!

So even before Harley's scooter – the Topper – was launched in mid-1959, there were two major problems: it was years too late and its manufacturer was perceived as being more connected to Hell's Angels than the humble scooterist.

Even so, from both historical (it was to be Harley-Davidson's only scooter) and a technical viewpoint, the Topper was an interesting addition to the scooter ranks.

From a design point of view, the machine was quite unusual. The horizontally mounted, beneath the floor, 164cc (60x58mm) two-stroke engine featured reed-valve induction, whilst needle rollers were employed for the big-end and main bearings. As the cylinder was faced forward, this, said Harley-Davidson, meant that a cooling fan was not needed. The transmission was automatic, by means of a Vee-belt primary drive carrying expanding pulleys, ratios being, again according to Harley-Davidson, 'infinitely variable' from 18:1 in the low range, to 6:1 at the top end. To start the engine, a pull handle, a similar device to one that would be found on a lawn-mower, was specified.

Its frame was a conventional steel tube affair whilst the bodywork was constructed of fibre-glass, and as one observer commented, 'with the two-tone paint scheme the Topper resembled a refrigerator on wheels'.

At the launch, two Topper models were

*Harley-Davidson arrived late on to the scooter scene – their Topper, with a 164cc reed-valve two-stroke engine, not appearing until mid-1959.*

*Various features of the Harley-Davidson D Topper from the official owner's handbook.*

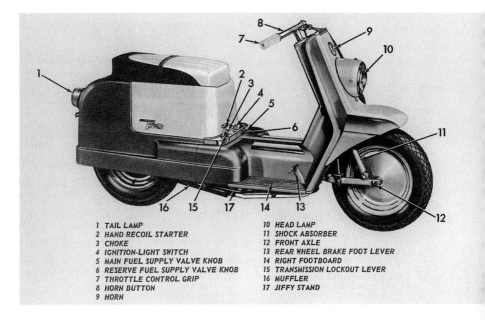

| | |
|---|---|
| 1 TAIL LAMP | 10 HEAD LAMP |
| 2 HAND RECOIL STARTER | 11 SHOCK ABSORBER |
| 3 CHOKE | 12 FRONT AXLE |
| 4 IGNITION-LIGHT SWITCH | 13 REAR WHEEL BRAKE FOOT LEVER |
| 5 MAIN FUEL SUPPLY VALVE KNOB | 14 RIGHT FOOTBOARD |
| 6 RESERVE FUEL SUPPLY VALVE KNOB | 15 TRANSMISSION LOCKOUT LEVER |
| 7 THROTTLE CONTROL GRIP | 16 MUFFLER |
| 8 HORN BUTTON | 17 JIFFY STAND |
| 9 HORN | |

offered: the A with 9.5bhp and the detuned AU, which only generated 5bhp and was equipped with a carburettor restrictor to comply with new state laws concerning minimum driving ages.

Then, in 1961, the Topper was updated, the A becoming the AH (also known as the H), whilst the AU version retained its original designation. But technically there was little or no change. And from then until the end of 1965, when production ceased, the Harley-Davidson scooter only received some new colour options.

The Topper was the only American scooter of the classic era that was available officially in Great Britain, small numbers coming in from the end of 1961, imported by F. W. Warr, priced in November 1961 at £257 2s 10d including British taxes.

## The American Scene

The American scooter scene was very different from the European one, but what did join the two was their youthful customer base. And with a few exceptions, notably the Harley-Davidson Topper, American scooter design was radically different from the European concept. In fact, as detailed earlier, the top-selling stateside 'scooters' were in fact best described as mini-motor cycles, with only their compact size and small-diameter wheels being the true scooter link.

# 7   The Eastern Bloc

This chapter could well have been entitled 'Iron Curtain' or even 'Soviet Bloc', as during the period covered by this book, Communist rule was very much a part of eastern Europe.

## Czechoslovakia

*Ceska Zbrojovka* (CZ) – the Czech Armament Works, did not commence motor cycle production until 1932, even though it had been first formed in 1918.

After 1945, CZ was merged with Jawa by the new Communist-controlled government (all industries were now state controlled, in common with all the areas under Soviet control). And it was thus the state, rather than the CZ management, which came up with the idea of producing a scooter.

## CZ Models

The prototype made its bow at the Prague Fair of 1946. This first design was powered by an air-cooled, single-cylinder two-stroke engine, with conventional piston-port induction.

In a most cost-effective manner, CZ was able to develop no fewer than three separate scooters from this original effort.

The first was the *Cezeta Bohéme*, which

*After the Second World War, the Czech CZ firm was merged with Jawa by the new Communist-controlled government. The first result of this marriage was the Cezeta Bohéme, with a 171.7cc (58x56mm) two-stroke engine. Its styling is best described as being 'cigar-like'.*

# Scooter MANET

also available in a royal blue/grey colour scheme

*THE FULL SIZED TWO-SEATER WITH AN ELECTRIC STARTER*

## LOOK AT THIS 10-STAR SPECIFICATION

★ 98cc 'square' two-stroke engine developing over 5 hp

★ Electric starter with 12v system and 2 batteries

★ Four-speed foot controlled gearbox, neutral selector

★ Built-in trafficators and steering lock

★ Screen, luggage carrier, dual seat standard equipment

★ 14 ins. wheels with full-width hubs

★ Centre and prop stands

★ 2 gallon tank with reserve

★ No extras to buy

★ Luxury two-wheeled transportation for two

## All this for only 114 gns. *(including £20.9.4. PT)*

### TECHNICAL DATA

**Engine**
Single cylinder 2-stroke fan cooled, alloy cylinder with liner, bore and stroke 50mm, 98.1cc, developing 5.1 hp at 5,500 rpm, compression ratio $7\frac{1}{2}$ : 1

**Clutch**
Four plate in oil bath

**Gearbox**
Four speed, foot operated with positive stop neutral selector

**Final Drive**
By fully enclosed chain

**Tyres**
3.00 x 14

**Suspension**
Front : by pivoted fork with coil spring and hydraulic damper. Rear : by pivoted fork with two coil springs and hydraulic damper.

**Brakes**
Internal expanding, in full-width hubs

**Electrical Equipment**
Headlamp with parking light, stop and tail light, 12v system with two 6v batteries, coil ignition, electric starter with AVC system

**Fuel Capacity**
Two gallons with reserve, filler under dual seat

**Dimensions**
Overall length 77.6″, overall width 22.6″, overall height (with screen) 55.1″, ground clearance 6.3″

**Weight**
Ready for road 243 lbs

**Standard Equipment**
Built-in trafficators, dual seat, windscreen, luggage carrier, centre stand, prop stand and steering lock

*Sold under the Jawa name in the UK by Industria, the 98cc Manet was a full-size scooter, helped by its large 14in wheels. Its comprehensive specification included a 12-volt electrical system with push-button starting.*

*Vintage Motor Scooter Club member Shaun Akroyd with his 1960 IWL Berlin SR59 with a 143cc engine.*

*The East German Simson KR51/1S Schwalbe with a 50cc engine producing 3.9bhp.*

benefited from a larger displacement – a 171.7cc (58x56mm) two-stroke engine breathing through a Kivov carburettor. However, there is no doubt that it was the highly unorthodox styling that was its outstanding feature – best described as being 'cigar-like'. The protruding nose served as a fuel tank above the front wheel, whilst a useful luggage carrier could be mounted on its face. No separate frame was

employed; instead, the body was constructed on the pressed-skin principle.

Next was the Manet, with a 98.1cc (50x50mm) fan-cooled engine developing 5.1bhp at 5,500rpm. The four-speed gearbox was foot operated with a positive-stop neutral finder. There was an oil-bath clutch, whilst the final drive was by a fully enclosed chain.

Sold under the Jawa brand name in Great

Britain by Industria of London, the Manet was a full-size scooter, with large 14in wheels, which were laced by spokes to full-width hubs. Other details of its comprehensive specification included an electric starter with a 12-volt system and two batteries, built-in trafficators, a screen, luggage carrier and dual seats as standard equipment.

There were also centre and side-stands, whilst the front suspension was by pivoted fork with a coil spring and hydraulic damper; at the rear things were kept under control thanks to a pivoted fork with two coil springs and a hydraulic damper.

Finally, during the mid-1960s the Manet became the Tatran, with a larger 124cc 7bhp engine size.

## East Germany

The East German scooter industry is confusing to say the least. First you have IFA, which became MZ (from 1955). Next was AWO which, like IFA/MZ, became Simson, and finally IWL. The latter organization built the Berlin scooter with a 143cc 9.5bhp MZ engine. Later this was updated, still with a 150 class engine, and was marketed as the Troll I, with more modern, squarer styling.

Later still came a whole range of Troll scooters, under the designations 60E, 100E, 120E and 120D. These were still being produced when the Berlin Wall came down at the beginning of the 1990s.

## The Soviet Union

The first Soviet scooter was announced in the summer of 1957 to a big fanfare of publicity.

Actually, there were *two* scooters, the Tula and the Vjatka. The Tula was by far the more popular and longer-lived. It was based, or rather copied, from the West German Glas Goggo 200 scooter (built in various forms from 1952 to 1956).

*The Soviet-built TGA-200F & K were 'cargo scooters' based on the Tula. All used a 199cc single-cylinder two-stroke engine.*

Coded T200, the Tula sported a 197cc (62x66mm) engine, equipped with an electric start, four-speed gearbox, 8bhp, front and rear suspension and 4.00x18 tyres. Maximum speed was in the region of 53mph (85km/h).

The T200 was built for many years and was

*Built by WFM, the Polish OSA M52 175cc scooter was a proven design having competed in the world-renowned International Six Days' Trial. Note the horizontal engine layout giving a low centre of gravity.*

revised as the Tula Tourist in 1973, but the first update had occurred as far back as 1959.

The TGA-200F and TGA-200K versions were also produced as scooter-trucks with a scooter front half (including the power unit) and a commercial box truck with two wheels at the rear. On these versions both an electric start and kick-starter were fitted. However, the maximum speed was reduced to 37mph (59.5km/h).

Exports of both the two and three-wheeled Tula scooters were handled by Autoexport of Moscow and shipments were despatched to many countries in Europe, Africa and the Middle East, plus of course fellow Communist bloc states.

## Poland

Manufactured by *Warszawska Fabryk Motocycli* (WFM), the OSA M52 175cc scooter was displayed for the first time in Great Britain at the Motor Cycle Show at Earls Court, London, in November 1964 by the Polish foreign trade enterprise Motoimport. Also on show were the SHL 175cc motor cycle and Komar moped.

The OSA scooter (also available with a 123cc engine unit), was a particularly well-proven design, having been successfully used competitively in the world's toughest motor cycle competition, the International Six Days' Trial (ISDT).

The OSA was equally suitable for road and cross-country travel – thanks in no small part to its use of large-diameter 14in tyres. The engine and chassis had begun in 1957 with a displacement of 149cc, three speeds and 6.5bhp at 5,000rpm. However, by the 1964 London Show, the engine size had been increased to 173cc and 8bhp at 4,800rpm – but still with three speeds, dry weight being 286lb (130kg).

## Hungary

Pannonia scooters and motor cycles were manufactured at the Mogürt factory in Budapest, sharing production lines with the Czepel Danuvia motor cycle range. The most notable scooter design was the R50, powered by a 48cc (38x42mm) single-cylinder two-stroke engine, with piston-port induction, producing 1.8bhp.

## Romania

Like the Polish WFM OSA, the Romanian URMW 150 scooter was introduced in 1957 and this was no coincidence, its 150cc engine featuring a horizontal cylinder and three-speed gearbox mounted in front of the rear wheel.

## Lack of Development

All Communist market transport products suffered from lack of development and innovation as time went by. Quite simply, with waiting lists stretching into years rather than months, all the countries reviewed in this chapter, to a greater or lesser extent, enjoyed a sellers' market. With virtually no competition there was little need to spend money on development. In addition, all the scooters thus produced had a requirement for servicing work to be carried out, if necessary, at the side of the road with few or no tools.

Of all the Communist countries, East Germany produced the best machines. Additionally, the Polish WFM OSA/Romania URMW 150, with their excellent off-road abilities and interesting horizontally mounted cylinder and rear-positioned gearbox were probably the most interesting from a technical viewpoint.

However, compared with modern western designs, the eastern bloc states could never have competed on a level playing field in a capitalist market.

# 8 Japan

## Fuji

Just as Piaggio with its Vespa brought the scooter to the masses in Italy, Fuji's Rabbit did the same in the Land of the Rising Sun.

Like Germany's, Japan's industrial heart had been bombed out of existence during the latter months of the Second World War. But even so, the Fuji Company saw the need, as in European countries, for economical transport. It introduced the first of its long series of Rabbit scooters in 1946, the same year as the first Vespas went into production on the other side of the globe. However, in that first year only eight Rabbits were constructed.

## The First Rabbits

The first model was an agricultural device with bodywork described by Michael Dregni as 'shaped more by a blacksmith than a designer'. This Fuji aped a style that was very much pre-war American scooter fashion. As was often the case in those days, this original model had no suspension, relying instead upon a heavily padded cushion to provide some basic comfort for the rider. A luggage rack was a standard fitment.

The highlight of the machine was that it employed a four-stroke engine that displaced 135cc (57x55mm), produced 2bhp at 3,000rpm and gave a top speed of 35mph (56km/h). Although not powerful, the Rabbit was exceedingly economical. By 1947 it was in mass production and every example was eagerly snapped up by a transport-starved public.

For the 1950 model year, Fuji produced an updated version, coded S23. This included several features that could, at that austere time, have been classed as luxuries: barrel-spring suspension, twin horns, a spare tyre and a padded pillion saddle.

## The S41 and S31

Later in 1950, two entirely new models were launched. The first to arrive was the Rabbit S41, using a bigger bore (61.5mm) version of the four-stroke engine, which had been enlarged to 170cc. Other notable features included 4.00x8 tyres and a power increase to 3bhp at 3,400rpm.

The other newcomer was the S31, the 'Jack Rabbit', which featured a longer wheelbase and what Michael Dregni described as 'a Cushman-like tail with luggage compartment'. For its time, the Jack Rabbit could best be described as a de luxe scooter, as it sported a twin-cylinder engine (a doubled-up 135cc Rabbit unit) that produced 4.5bhp at 3,500rpm.

Production of these models continued until 1954 when they were replaced by the more modern-looking and more powerful S48 and S61.

## The S48 and S61

The S48 engine was based on the outgoing S41, but with a longer stroke of 67mm, giving a displacement of 199cc and producing a claimed 5bhp at 3,000rpm. The S61 was the top-of-the-range model, with not only a larger 225cc engine capacity and 5.9bhp at

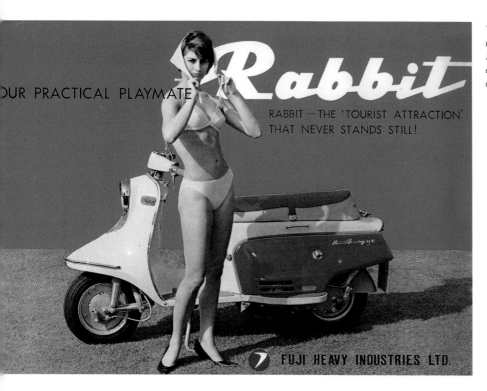

OUR PRACTICAL PLAYMATE

*Rabbit*

RABBIT — THE 'TOURIST ATTRACTION'
THAT NEVER STANDS STILL!

FUJI HEAVY INDUSTRIES LTD.

*The Rabbit scooter range was manufactured by Fuji. The S402BT employed a 150cc engine with a rotary valve and electric start.*

4,000rpm, but luxury features, including an electric start.

The styling of both newcomers was a quantum leap in Japanese scooter design of the period, and showed the tremendous progress being made by the domestic two-wheeled industry. The role played by the Japanese motor cycle manufacturers has been well documented, but that of its scooter producers has up to now been virtually ignored.

Besides the actual styling, Fuji had given their latest scooters a certain edge, but the use of bright trim-work and also, even a début of the marque's circular chrome Rabbit logo – a feature which was to remain on future models.

**More New Models**
From then on, Fuji's development team seemed to be constantly bringing out new models and changes to existing ones.

In 1955, a smaller 125cc (52x58mm)

model, the S71 Rabbit, was produced and for 1957 it was revamped as the S72 with bodywork revisions that saw additional chrome trim and air ducts for the side panels. Then, in 1958, the S82 made its début, putting out 6.2bhp at 5,600rpm – the previous 125 engine producing 5bhp at 5,000rpm. This was updated again for the 1960 model year as the S82S.

**The Superflow**
In 1957, the S101 Rabbit Superflow superseded the S61. An interesting feature of the Superflow was its torque converter automatic transmission and a displacement of 249cc (68.5x67mm), giving 5.9bhp at 4,000rpm. Michael Dregni commented that, 'Bells and whistles were everywhere on the Superflow: electric start, front and rear turn signals, instrument dashboard with gas gauge and warning light that lit at excessive riding speeds, parking

brake, foot-operated headlamp dimmer, and stylish two-tone paint.'

An improved version of the Superflow was offered for 1959, coded S100 D2. The changes included improved, cleaner styling and an increase in power output to 7bhp at 4,000rpm, but the actual engine size remained unchanged.

In 1961, Fuji introduced a 50cc scooter, which sported a single saddle and simple styling. Its 49cc engine put out 3bhp and was equipped with 3.00x10 tyres. Also introduced in that year was the 125cc 5300; which was updated for 1962 as the S301 – using similar styling to the Superflow model. By 1965, the 125cc engine had been increased in size to 149cc.

## Moped-Scooters

Fuji, like many other Japanese manufacturers, also produced a series of what are best described as moped-scooters. All of these were prompted by the hugely successful Honda Super Cub that had arrived in 1958 and was destined to become the world's top-selling powered two-wheeler (by the 21st century, sales worldwide had topped 30 million and are still rising).

## The Mid-1960s

By the mid-1960s the Fuji range of scooters comprised the Rabbit 90, the Rabbit Touring 150 and the Rabbit Superflow S601. The latter, powered by a fan-cooled 199cc (65x60mm) single-cylinder, two-stroke engine could reach 60mph (96.5km/h) from 11bhp at 5,500rpm. There was both electric and kick-starting.

The electrical equipment comprised a pair of 6-volt 18-amp hour batteries in series for the 12-volt system needed to operate the electric start. And like earlier Superflows there was an hydraulic torque converter. Other details of the S601's specification included leading-link front forks with hydraulic damping, swinging-arm rear suspension, 4.00x8 tyres, split wheel rims and a dry weight of 337lb (153kg).

*The Rabbit Superflow S601 with a 199cc (65x60mm) engine producing 11bhp and capable of 60mph (96.5km/h).*

*Rabbit* **SCOOTER**

The newest model features a rotary-valve engine, four speeds, hand clutch and a pushbutton electric starter. The S402BT (150 cc) is equipped with a soft-as-silk dual seat. This dynamically-styled RABBIT is available in a contrasting color combination.

Go farther — go faster — go with a free frame of mind — GO RABBIT! It GETS you places! It lends luxury to any landscape. Get the habit of riding a Rabbit!

*The Rabbit and Mitsubishi's Pigeon series were Japan's top-selling scooters.*

Fuji Heavy Industries now had no fewer than eight plants, two of which, Mitaka and Gumma, produced scooters. Fuji was yet another large engineering organization that saw the benefits of the scooter for its financial health in the immediate aftermath of the Second World War, but continued to produce the small-wheeled vehicles even after its corporate fortunes had been restored.

Fuji produced more units than all other Japanese manufacturers combined, if one discounts Honda's Super Cub (which in reality was not a scooter in the true sense).

## Mitsubishi

Mitsubishi was the other leading Japanese scooter manufacturer. Like Piaggio, Mitsubishi had been a major aircraft supplier during the Second World War. In fact, with its famous Zero fighter (the mainstay of the Japanese

Navy's air force during the conflict), Mitsubishi outshone Piaggio in aircraft production figures by a considerable margin. Mitsubishi marketed its scooter series under the Pigeon brand name and, together with the Fuji Rabbit family, the two firms were very much the Vespa and Lambretta of the Far East.

As in Italy, scooter production in Japan grew rapidly. In 1946, only eight scooters (all Fuji) were built, but by 1954, more than 450,000 were on the roads of Japan with the country's total production running at 50,000 annually. And by 1958, this had rocketed to 113,218.

### The First Pigeons

As with Fuji's first scooter, Mitsubishi's entry into the scooter field, in 1948, with its 115cc two-stroke C11 model, was a pretty basic effort. And in this case it borrowed many of its styling and design features from an American scooter, the mid-1930s Motor Glide. The engine had bore and stroke dimensions of 57x44mm. With a lowly power output of 1.5bhp at 3,500rpm, top speed was 31mph (50km/h). Tyre size was equally puny – 3.50x5in.

The following year, the machine was revamped as the C13, but was still pretty basic.

### The C21, C22 and C35

As the 1950s dawned, in direct response to customer demand, the Pigeon series was expanded to include new designs with larger engines. The initial, 'cheap and cheerful, anything will do' attitude would no longer suffice as the customers became more sophisticated – a demand that was to increase as the decade unfolded.

The first of the new breed, the C21, was introduced in 1950 and was equipped with a 150cc (57x58mm) engine, producing 3bhp at 3,800rpm. Not only was a pillion seat made available, but also a tradesman-type sidecar for commercial purposes.

In 1951 the C22 replaced the C21, this having a more glitzy image thanks to its use of air ducts over almost every available space of the tail section. Then, in 1953, the C35 model arrived with not only a four-stroke engine, but also three speeds and 8in tyres.

### The C57, C57II and C90

For the 1954 season, Mitsubishi engineers gave their Pigeon range new styling. At the top came a new 200cc (65x58mm) model, coded C57, with a four-stroke powerplant putting out 4.3bhp at 3,800rpm. Other innovations included wider 4.00 section tyres (still 8in), and automatic transmission. As for the styling itself, this was a curious blend of curves and the previous Pigeon square section approach, set off with an abundance of chrome plate, direction indicators, enclosed handlebars – and again a vast array of air ducts in the rear bodywork.

The C57II arrived in 1956 with more

brightwork, but little other change. Then in 1957 a new 200-engined model made its bow in the shape of the sleekly styled C90.

### Copying Lambretta

During 1955 the 125 was updated by blatantly copying the Italian Lambretta LC model, even down to the trio of port-holes on the side covers. At that time there existed widespread duplication of western design by Japanese industry. But as far as it is known, none of the manufacturers wronged, which included not only Lambretta, but also Triumph, BSA Sunbeam and AMC, ever took legal redress.

The Lambretta copy came with a new 124cc (55x52.5mm) two-stroke engine that produced 3.6bhp, with three speeds and 4.00x18 tyres.

The Lambretta styling was retained on the C73 of 1958–59, which was followed by the 192cc C74 four-stroke. Then the four-stroke 125cc C83 ran alongside the existing C73 two-stroke – with lines that were clearly poached from the newly released Lambretta TV1!

The C83 was given the rather curious Bobby de Luxe tag – and likewise the Peter de Luxe of 1959, powered by a 210cc four-stroke unit.

### More New Models

By now it was becoming increasingly difficult to keep up with developments being introduced by Mitsubishi's scooter arm. During 1960, the C110 175cc and C111 210cc scooter arrived, both with ohv engines and massive-looking Maico Mobil-type front ends.

And so development continued apace. 1963 saw a redesign of the 125cc model as the C135 Silver Pigeon with curvaceous, modern styling and 8bhp. In 1964 the 125 was facelifted as the C140 and the four-speed C240 150cc made its bow.

## Stateside Imports

American imports of Mitsubishi scooters were handled by the Rockford Scooter Company of Illinois. These were marketed in the USA as the Rockford range of scooters in Special, de Luxe and Custom variants, and as the Silver Pigeon. Rockford also wholesaled machines to Montgomery Ward, who sold them by mail order as Riversides – very confusing both then and now. Models imported into the USA included the C73, C74, C76 and C90 models.

# Honda

As the world knows, Soichiro Honda was a legend in his own lifetime, and for a very good reason. He not only created the most successful motor cycle marque in history, but he did so by rewriting the motor cycle industry 'handbook'.

Beginning in 1946 with an auxiliary-engined bicycle, Honda progressed via the A-type engine (1947) and the B-type motor cycle (1948) to the D-type Dream (1949). From then on, Honda found it difficult to get things wrong, and its early reputation was built very much on producing high-quality models with class-leading performance, a degree of technical innovation unmatched by its competitors, and value for money. But of course, as other motor cycle manufacturers found to their cost, scooters were an entirely different ball game – so why did Honda produce scooters? Well, the answer is pretty simple – it was inspired by the success in this sector of Fuji's Rabbit and Mitsubishi's Pigeon.

## The Juno KA and KB

In 1954 Honda introduced its first small-wheeled device, the Juno KA. This employed an 189cc (65x57mm) overhead-valve, four-stroke engine, which produced 5bhp at 4,800rpm. The transmission used three speeds with foot-change, geared primary drive and an enclosed final drive chain. Interestingly, the KA scooter

*Honda's first scooter, the Juno K-type of 1954. However, the Juno, built in various guises for over a decade, never challenged either Fuji or Mitsubishi.*

was the first Honda-designed engine not to feature square bore and stroke dimensions.

The KA was only produced in one colour, mist-green metallic – not far removed from the early Vespa green. It featured two separate seats, enclosed handlebars and a headlamp built into the windshield pressing. There were leading-link front forks, swinging-arm rear suspension with twin shock absorbers, and 9in pressed steel split wheels. But although it had a remarkably impressive specification, the KA at around 350lb (159kg) dry was simply too heavy for the power available.

Because of this, the KA was replaced the following year by the KB. This was essentially the same basic machine, but with the engine capacity increased to 219cc, by increasing the bore size to 70mm (the stroke remained unchanged at 57mm). But most important of all, the power output was increased to 9bhp at 5,500rpm. Maximum speed was 55mph (88km/h).

## The Juno M80

In 1960 came the brand-new M80 powered by a 124.99 (43x43mm) overhead-valve horizontally opposed twin-cylinder power unit featuring variable transmission. Producing

10bhp, the new Honda scooter was kitted out with a host of luxury accessories as standard – direction indicators, an electric start, a glove box, a fuel gauge and much, much more.

Compared with the earlier attempts, the newcomer was a much more sophisticated piece of machinery. As for the styling, this was not to everyone's taste, Michael Dregni commenting that 'the elements never quite fit together, looking like a toolroom special made up of not just Honda spare parts but parts from every other Japanese scooter make as well. Even the flashy, two-tone paint could not save the lack of styling.'

Strangely, the most serious mistake Honda made with the M80 was its lack of power-to-weight ratio. But this was more from a torque viewpoint than actual outright performance. Put simply, it needed to be revved hard to get anywhere. Potential scooter buyers were not impressed.

### The Juno M85

And so, for the 1962 season, Honda engineers uprated the flat twin, enlarging the engine displacement to 168.9cc by boring out the cylinders to 50mm. With a compression ratio of 8.5:1, power output was 12bhp at 7,600rpm. But the big improvement was in flexibility.

The revised machine was coded M85 and retained the Juno tag. Like the earlier M80 model, what really set it apart was the transmission: a hydraulic device incorporating a swash plate pump and motor, providing infinitely variable gearing (controlled by the nearside twist-grip) between limits of 21.75 and 6.25:1. (Actually, the origins of the hydraulic transmission were not Japanese but Italian, having been devised by the Rome-based Baldini concern.)

It had no clutch in the conventional manner. Instead, the conventional lever on the handlebar operated a bypass valve, allowing the pump to rotate without transmitting oil pres-

sure to the motor but, for most purposes, the lever could be totally ignored.

In practice, the M85 Juno was simplicity itself. A touch of the starter button of the 12-volt system brought the scooter to life, and the only precaution necessary prior to moving off was to check that the nearside grip was wound forward to the 'low' position. From then on it was merely a matter of opening the throttle as the scooter took up its drive. As one tester of the era described, 'there is a fascination of holding the throttle position steady and varying the scooter's speed with the gear grip. And I've never ridden anything so uncannily smooth.'

The M85's production life only lasted until 1964, after which Honda concentrated on its motor cycle and moped ranges, plus, of course, its four-wheeled activities.

However, for once the mighty Honda corporation could not win a market, even though it had offered the most technically advanced products.

### Other Marques

Besides Fuji, Mitsubishi and Honda, several other marques built and sold scooters during the period covered by this book. These were Hirano (1950s and early 1960s), Sanko Kogyo (1950s), Showa (late 1950s), Swallow (1955–late 1950s) and Yamaha (1960). The latter's offerings were the SC1, powered by a 175cc (62x58mm) single-cylinder two-stroke engine and the MF1 50cc ultra-lightweight moped-scooter. But neither proved popular and they were soon discontinued. Yamaha, like Honda, did not build any more scooters until the 1980s. As for Suzuki and Kawasaki, they only ever produced scooter-moped hybrids during this time.

So, as with the Italian scooter industry, two firms, Fuji and Mitsubishi, dominated the Japanese scene, whilst even the mighty Honda was only a sideshow in the scooter league.

# 9  Scooter Sport

Anyone who thinks scooters and sport don't mix would be very wrong. In fact, the world-wide scooter boom of the immediate post-war period saw a parallel explosion of the scooter's use in all forms of competition. Lambretta and Vespa went head-to-head in record breaking for both speed and endurance.

## Lambretta – Distance and Speed

During 1950 and 1951, Lambretta broke a number of distance and speed records. The engine they chose for this task was a specially prepared version of their 52x58mm 125cc unit. To ensure that enough power would be available, it was decided to fit a supercharger, this being mounted on the nearside (left), where the magneto normally went. As for the magneto, this was discarded in favour of a simple battery/coil system. The cylinder barrel, piston and head, plus the bottom end were very similar to the production engine – even the three-speed twist-grip gear change was retained. The clutch featured an additional plate to cope with the extra power, reputed to have been 13.5bhp at 9,000rpm. The fuel was a special brew with a methanol base, whilst the exhaust was constructed to suit the supercharger. But it was the frame and streamlining which were the biggest innovations, as the photographs show.

### Saving the Best for Last

Most magnificent of all the record attempts by Lambretta was the last of the series. For this Lambretta chose motor cycle racing star

Romolo Ferri, who was congratulated by Viktor Frankenburg of NSU (whose company built Lambrettas under licence from 1951–56) after Ferri had smashed five world records on 10 August 1951. The venue for this attempt was a section of the Munich–Ingolstadt *Autobahn* in West Germany. This included covering the flying start kilometre in 17.95 seconds, a speed equal to 125mph (201km/h).

Earlier, Ferri had been part of a three-man team (the others being Ambrosini and Rizzi) who, on 5 October 1950, at Montlhéry, in France had shattered the 621-mile (1,000km),

*During 1950 and 1951, Lambretta broke a number of distance and speed records. The engine was a supercharged version of the 125 production unit – the real innovation was in the chassis and streamlining.*

six-hour and twelve-hour records with speeds of 82.34mph (132.48km/h), 82.59mph (132.88km/h) and 82.34mph (132.48km/h) respectively.

### Lambretta Versus MV Agusta

If record breaking was not serious enough, Lambretta also took on the might of MV Agusta in the scooter-racing competitions of the early 1950s, both companies building specialized racing mounts. Lambretta produced two-strokes exclusively, but MV Agusta fielded both two- and four-stroke versions. Displacing 125cc these tiny speed machines were capable of approaching 90mph (145km/h) and had all the technology of pukka Grand Prix racing motor cycles, but with small wheels!

### Vespa Fights Back

Naturally, Lambretta's main competitor, Vespa, couldn't simply sit back and let its chief rival take all the glory. On 9 February 1951, the specially constructed Vespa Streamliner, ridden by works tester Mazzoncini, broke the 125cc world speed record at well over 100mph (161km/h) on the Rome–Ostia *autostrada*. But this was, unlike the Lambretta efforts, achieved with a one-off 123cc (42.9x44mm) twin-cylinder, water-cooled two-stroke engine. However, the Vespa did not employ a supercharger to obtain its claimed 18bhp at 9,600rpm. Running on methanol, the compression ratio was 11:1. There were two racing Dell'Orto carburettors and the machine weighed in (dry) at 205lb (93kg). The entire ignition system, together with the aluminium

*Motor Cycle Grand Prix star Romolo Ferri being congratulated by NSU director Viktor Frankenburg after setting five new world speed records on August 10 1951 with his Lambretta Streamliner.*

streamlined shell, was produced by Piaggio themselves.

## The ISDT

Both Lambretta and Vespa entered scooters in the famous International Six Days' Trial (ISDT) – the Olympics of the two-wheeled world during the early 1950s. Competing against motor cycles from all over the world, the Italian small-wheeled devices did far better than anyone could have imagined. The 1951 event was staged on Italian soil, in the north of the country, and both Vespa and Lambretta entered manufacturer's teams. The Piaggio 'C' Vespa team won a special award with no marks lost, the riders being Merlo, Riva and Romano. FIM Gold Medals (the highest award in the trial) were won by Mazzoncini (125 Vespa), Opessi (125 Vespa), Granchi (125 Vespa), Merlo (125 Vespa), Can (125 Vespa), Masserini (125 Lambretta), Nesti (125 Vespa), Riva (125 Vespa), Vivaldi (125 Vespa) and Romano (125 Vespa).

*Motor Cycle* dated 27 September 1951 carried the headline 'Very Fast Scooters', going on to say, 'Many of these scooters, incidentally, having been achieving speeds of about 70mph.

*Strangely, Lambretta's biggest challenger in road racing was not Vespa, but MV Agusta, the latter building racing scooters with both two-stroke (as shown) and four-stroke engines.*

*Rivals Vespa responded by building a 125cc water-cooled twin-cylinder Streamliner that put out 18bhp and could easily exceed 100mph (161km/h).*

One of the reasons for this success was that they were using alcohol fuel – and mixing with it with a castor-based oil!'

## Rumi and The *Bol d'Or*

During the late 1950s, Rumi enjoyed considerable success with its 125 *Formichino* in the French *Bol d'Or* 24-hour endurance motor cycle race. Developed from the standard model, the Sport versions were works-entered. In 1956, the Sports category was won by a Rumi piloted by Cambis and Ditail, averaging 44.34mph (71.34km/h) even though they had to spend some unscheduled time in the pits along the way.

This was the first in a series of Rumi successes in this legendary event. In 1957, Rumi gained the top two places in the Racing Category, competing against machines of up to 175cc. Then in 1958, a new 125cc class had been created and Rumi achieved the best-ever performance by a scooter in the *Bol d'Or*, when Bois and Foidell covered a distance of 1,302 miles (2,095 km) at an average speed of 54.25mph (87.28km/h).

*The Vespa Streamliner in action in February 1951 on the Rome–Ostia autostrada.*

172

*A Lambretta 125 competing in the 1951 International Six Days Trial, which was held in Italy that year.*

In recognition of this feat, Rumi produced a high-performance production model, appropriately named *Bol d'Or*. Finished in a striking white and gold, it could achieve almost 80mph (129km/h). Besides the speed and distance record breaking, road racing, endurance racing and trials, scooters were used for virtually every other form of two-wheeled sport, including grass track, sand racing, hill-climbing, motocross and sprinting.

Scooter clubs had boomed during the 1950s and although they mainly concerned themselves with the social side of the movement and with running gymkanas and rallies, as the machines became larger and more powerful, scooters took part in all sorts of more serious sporting activities.

## The Manx Rally

The National Scooter Association (NSA) was not in favour of racing, but nonetheless they teamed up with the Manx Tourist Board and in 1957 a National Scooter Rally (more commonly known simply as the Manx Rally)

*The Rumi Formichino, a big success during the late 1950s, winning the French Bol d'Or 24-hour race on more than one occasion.*

173

*Sand racing on the beach at Douglas, Isle of Man during Scooter Week, circa 1969.*

*A trio of Heinkel Tourists, taking part in a regularity event in West Germany, circa 1959.*

was held on the Isle of Man. Although this first event was a relatively modest affair, this could certainly not be said of the second year's gathering – now named the World Scooter Rally, with an FIM international permit and a full week-long programme. An entry of over 200 included not only club members from all over Europe, but also Tourist Trophy (TT) stars such as Freddie Frith and Denis Parkinson.

The track events ranged from a one-lap of the 37.73-mile (60.7km) TT course, to a 24-hour regularity test for teams of two riders per machine. Despite appalling weather conditions, the Bond team, on scooters that had only recently entered the market, took the team prize.

Other events that week included a 'point-to-point', which was more akin to motocross, the National Assembly Rally (longest distances travelled), plus concours and Scooter King and Queen contests.

For the 1959 Manx Rally, entries were up again and rules for the long-distance events tightened up.

The Isle of Man Scooter Association's 1960 Concours drew 179 entries. The change of name from 'Rally' to 'Concours' was insisted upon by the FIM, which reserved the title for an event of its own.

Back under its former title, the Manx Scooter Rally, the 1961 meeting was affected by bad weather. And so things continued, with the Isle of Man Scooter week continuing throughout the remainder of the 1960s – even though scooter sales had declined drastically as the decade unfolded.

## Scooters At The Palace

The first-ever scooter race on the British mainland was staged at the South London Crystal Palace circuit on Saturday 2 July 1960, organized by the British Motor Cycle Racing Club. As *Motor Cycle* reported, 'A sparkling variety of machinery turned out … they

*UK scooter racing was popular during the 1960s; the first such event was staged at Crystal Palace, London on 2 July 1960.*

ranged from 50cc moped-engined miniatures to massive Vincent-powered sidecar outfits. There were scooters too – taking part in a special event and with their panelling and weather shielding looking more ready for a *concours d'elegance* than a road race.'

But race they did, over six laps, with victory eventually going to J. B. Gamble (277cc Maicoletta), Don Noys (174cc Heinkel) and M. D. Brown (145cc Vespa). The Heinkel Tourist piloted by Don Noys into second place was the very same machine on which Peter Humber had won the scooter class of the Welsh Two-Day Trial a few weeks before, displaying the versatility of the machine.

## The Publicity Machine

Quite often the scooter was used in sporting events to gain publicity, as they stood out when the majority were on motor cycles. The Lambretta British sales manager, Alan Kimber, competed in several major trials during the early 1960s, one of the then-new James 150

MAIN FACTORY BUILDING

INTERNATIONAL SCOOTER RALLY, MONTE-CARLO
6 Terrots at start, 6 at finish, winning International Trophy for highest in. p. g.

TERROT & C⁰ DIJON (France)

DISTRIBUTORS :

*Factory brochure showing the French Terrot works team at the International Scooter Rally in Monte Carlo during the mid-1950s. Six started, six finished.*

scooters gained several awards in Midlands trials following its launch in 1960, whilst salesman-turned-racer Walt Fulton rode a souped-up Mustang to many successes during the early 1950s – even beating the massive Harley-Davidson and Indian vee-twin motor cycles on several occasions, whilst the Polish OSA gained gold medals in the ISDT.

During 1950–51, Innocenti even created a 250cc (54x54mm) dohc vee-twin Grand Prix racing motor cycle. The 29bhp machine, designed by Pierluigi Torre, was created as a warning to the Italian motor cycle industry that if they attempted to enter the scooter scene, Innocenti was quite able – and willing – to take them on at their own game.

# 10 Today's Classic Scooter Scene

*Gunter Harr ran the Heinkel (West Germany) scooter club branch in Heilbronn-Bockingen during the 1980s.*

Since the mid-1980s there has been a massive explosion of interest in the classic scooter. And this has come not just from those who owned one of the machines during the period, but also from an entirely new breed of riders – ones who were not even born when scooters were being ridden in the 1950s and 1960s. So why has this happened? Well, the answer is really nostalgia – a longing for or sentimental recollection of the past. Of course, this phenomenon is not just restricted to the scooter world, it can be found in virtually every other form of transportation. But what makes the scooter a special case is all the things that surround it, best described as a 'cult'.

Today, there are a vast array of products aimed at the scooter owner or enthusiast, including clubs and museums, restorations, tuning, customizing and replacement parts, plus books, magazines, DVDs, calendars, even time-themed clocks! Whatever someone may need in the classic scooter world, someone is providing that item or service. It is very much a case of demand leading to supply.

## Clubs

The scooter club scene is every bit as popular as it was during the heyday of the late 1950s, with organizations not just in the UK, but in Australia, Austria, Belgium, Canada, Denmark, Finland, France, Germany, Gibraltar, Holland, Indonesia, Ireland, Italy, Japan, Malaysia, New

# The VMSC

The Vintage Motor Scooter Club (VMSC)) was formed in 1985 to cater for the needs of scooter enthusiasts interested in the preservation and restoration of all makes and models of motor scooters. Who would have thought back in September 1985, when an inaugural meeting was held, quickly followed by a Committee meeting on 3 November 1986, that this somewhat unfashionable club would grow to a membership of over 800, mainly in the UK but with some members in continental Europe, Nordic, the USA and New Zealand to name but a few, and to have a reputation second to none in the scootering world. Speaking of that first Committee meeting, a number of those early pioneers still serve on it, this small band being supplemented with other enthusiastic and devoted individuals, who have continually moved the club forward.

The club is run on democratic principals, via an elected Committee, and has an ethos of giving something back to its members, evidenced by an array of giveaways including a limited-edition pewter scooter model, volumes 1–3 of its highly acclaimed road test books, and various other items, including an annual year planner. In addition to these items, members receive six club magazines throughout the year containing articles on members' experiences, technical items, 'wants and sales' and other valuable information. The magazine provides members with the opportunity to network with others who have similar machines and can therefore share knowledge, spares and experiences. A major attraction of the club is the access members enjoy to unrivalled expertise on most scooters ever produced, with many members owning numerous scooters, and most marques and models have at least one expert who can be consulted.

Members of the club own and ride a vast range of scooter models, some of which never came to full production, and are therefore of immense historic value in the history of motor scooters.

A packed calendar is available to all members and their families, events comprising three excellent traditional camping weekends held around the country. These weekends give owners and enthusiasts the chance to meet and socialize, and in a throwback to the heyday of scooter clubs, ride out as a group, to the usual amazement and admiration of the general public.

The club also has representation at many major shows and exhibitions, including the prestigious International Classic Motor Cycle Show in Stafford. Another key event for the VMSC is its 'Extravaganza', which has now found a home at the excellent Sports Connexion facility in Coventry, and is regarded as one of the top shows in the UK, regularly attracting large crowds and some of the best vintage and customized machines in the country. The show increases in size and popularity year on year, and enjoys sponsorship from a number of high-profile organizations in the scootering world.

Club membership is open to anyone with an interest in motor scooters, be they owners or not, and a warm and friendly welcome is guaranteed for prospective members.

Brian Crook
VMSC

Zealand, Norway, The Philippines, Portugal, Russia, Singapore, South Africa, Spain, Sweden, Switzerland, Thailand, the USA and Vietnam. Amazing!

In the UK alone there are almost 600 scooter clubs and new clubs are forming all the time. Some, like the Vespa Club of Great Britain (*see* Chapter 1) have been around for over fifty years, whilst the Vintage Motor Scooter Club caters for all makes. Others specialize in a single brand, or for the local scooterist, in a particular town or city.

As for names, well, here's a selection: 'The Odd Mod Squad', 'Mad Mods & English Men', 'Exit 17', 'Shabbylads', 'The Tin Soldiers', 'Silver Torqued Cavaliers', 'Spalding Tulips', 'Gatecrashers', 'Nifty 50s', 'Blue and Gold', 'God's A Mod', 'Despicable Donkey', 'The Scoots of Hazard', 'Cloud 9' and 'Destination Unknown'. Some even have a movie theme – 'Jurassic Parka's', 'Sid James' and 'Friends of Oliver Reed', whilst probably the longest is, 'Dip Me in Chocolate and Feed me to the Cheerleaders'!

## Restoration

During the 1970s, many scooters were simply laid up in garages, sheds, barns and the like. Some even stood, forlornly abandoned outside the owner's home. Then came the re-birth, both for new scooter sales, with the latest twist-and-go designs, and the nostalgia boom. The latter meant, in most cases, serious restoration work. Although these were mainly Vespas and Lambrettas, a surprisingly large number of other scooter makes survived from the 1950s and 1960s, notably the German designs, many of which had been considered almost over-engineered in their day, but whose quality meant that a large proportion had survived.

Even now, scooters are being restored all around the globe. Some are rebuilt painstakingly to the original specification by dedicated enthusiasts and specialist dealers, whilst others are restored in a non-standard state according to the taste of their particular owner.

*This 1957 Lambretta LDA 150 was photographed by the author at the Edinburgh Show Ground Classic Exhibition, August 2004.*

## Customizing

The scooter customizing world is vast; there just seems an unending number of 'goodies' with which to decorate your machine and an almost equally large number of firms wishing to provide these components. Again, items for Vespas and Lambrettas dominate, but that's not to say you can't find the odd specialist who can provide bits for other marques.

There are even painting, stainless steel, carbon fibre, engraving and chroming-only firms. And of course the end results of all this hard work – and much expense – are some truly outstanding examples of scooter art. All this only adds to the enthusiasm displayed by owners and the general public alike.

## Tuning

Tuning is another important aspect of the classic scooter scene, for engines and chassis improvements alike. And this has a positive slant, as modern road traffic requires better performance and braking than was ever the case during the immediate post-war years.

Some of the most popular components include 250cc kits for 200 Series Lambrettas,

*The author's friend Derek Farrar in spring 2007 with his superbly restored 1960 Dürkopp Diana Sport.*

*A rare 1959 Mercury 98cc Pippin, one of only a few models built, on display at the VMSC Stand, Stafford, April 2007.*

181

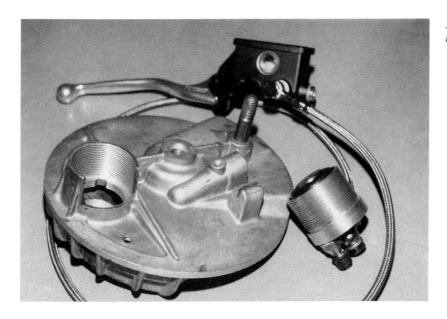

*An hydraulic disc brake conversion for a Lambretta.*

*1970 Lambretta GP200 with 225 Rapido big-bore kit. Owner Steve Justice is pictured at Cadwell Park in 2007.*

hydraulic disc brake conversions, rev counters, gas shocks, electronic ignition, modern carburettors, expansion chamber exhaust systems, carbon fibre panels, cowls and much, much more.

As an example, you could get into some really serious engine work including blueprinting racing components such as the crankshaft and piston, close ratio-gear clusters and special clutches. But it is always important to remember that the engine characteristics need to be suitable for the intended use. Obviously, for track use the sky's the limit, providing you have plenty of cash to throw at the project, whereas for street use it needs to be above all tractable. Tuned two-strokes need to be kept detonation-free so some riders, even for the road use avgas (aviation high octane fuel) and a premium grade high-performance oil for their tuned engines.

## Museums

There are even museums dedicated purely to scooters. I have visited ones in the UK,

*Steve Bond (in centre of trio) and his Zündapp Bella R204 (with an R154 body); he rides his machine on a daily basis. To Steve's right is Neil Powell who until recently owned over ninety-two classic scooters; whilst on the left is Eddie Weeks who was a Bella owner when they were first released in the UK; circa mid-1950s.*

Germany and Italy and found them all really interesting.

Sometimes you will find the really rare and unusual. For example at the Lambretta and Scooter Museum in Rodano, the sole remaining prototype (two were originally constructed) of Lambretta's 1967 Project 137 twin-cylinder 200cc (50x50mm) is to be found. This superb engine was the work of two designers, Ugo Malter and Sandro Colombo. Although extremely promising, it was never put into production due to the rapidly dwindling scooter sales that occurred towards the end of the 1960s. However, it is worth noting that the Project 137 twin got as far as being presented to the Italian press – and a test session at Monza Autodrome was witnessed by the head of the British Lambretta importers, Peter Agg. But besides falling sales, there was also the problem of the twin being some 25 per cent more expensive than the then-current top of the range 5x200 single.

Consequently, the twin never reached production.

## What of The Future?

So what of the future for the classic scooter? Well, just as with classic motor cycles and classic cars, the current level of interest is extremely healthy. Whether this will remain so is more difficult to forecast. However, much depends upon new, younger enthusiasts joining the existing ownership circle. Scooters have always been seen as 'cool' – a youth culture – closely linked to celebrities and pop stars. This was something Piaggio cleverly worked on over fifty years ago – and it remains the case today. So I am quietly confident.

Probably the classic scooter's biggest trump card is the comradeship enjoyed by its enthusiastic owners. The culture and the family aspect of scooters cannot be over-estimated.

183

# Appendix
# World Scooter Manufacturers 1945–70

ABC Scootamota, GB (1920–21)
Achilles, West Germany (1953–57)
ACMA Vespa, France (1950–62)
Adler, West Germany (1955–57)
Aermacchi, Italy (1950–63)
AGF, France (1951–52)
Agrati-Garelli, Italy (1958–67)
Aldimi, Belgium (1953–56)
Allstate, USA (1951–63)
Alpino, Italy (1952–60)
Ambassador, GB (early 1960s)
Ambrosini, Italy (1952)
AMO, West Germany (1955)
Ardent, France (1951–53)
Argyle Scooter Cub (*see* C & E
    Manufacturing)
Ariel, GB (1958–65)
Auto-Glide, USA (*see* Cushman)
Autoglider, GB (1919–21)
Autoped, USA (1915–21)
Autosco, GB (1920)
Avro (*see* Roe)
AWO (*see* Simson)

Baby-moto, France (1951–52)
Bambi, Italy (early 1950s)
Bangor Scootmaster, USA (late 1930s)
Basert, West Germany (1952–56)
Beam, USA (late 1940s)
Beckmann, West Germany (1953)

Benelli, Italy (early–mid-1960s)
Berlin (*see* IWL)
Bernardet, France (1947–59)
Bianchi, Italy (1960–65)
Binz, West Germany (mid-1950s)
Bitri, Holland (1954–early 60s)
BMW, West Germany (1954, prototype only)
Bond, GB (1950–62)
Britax, GB (early 1950s)
Brockhouse, GB (1946–52)
BSA, GB (1955–65)
Buydens, Belgium (1951–52)

C & E Manufacturing, USA (1960s)
Capri (*see* Agrati-Garelli)
Carnielli, Italy (early 1950s)
Casalini, Italy (1958–59)
Casel, Portugal (1960s–70s)
Cazenave, France (1954–61)
Cimatti, Italy (early 1960s)
Cityfix (*see* Delius)
Claeys-Flandria, Belgium (1950s–60s)
Clark Engineering, USA (1940s)
Columbus Cycle, USA (1960s)
Comet, USA (1930s)
Como, Italy (*see* Agrati-Garelli)
Condor, Switzerland (mid-1950s–early 60s)
Corgi (*see* Brockhouse)
Cosmo, USA/Italy (late 1950s)
Cresent, Sweden (1950s–60s)

Crocker, USA (late 1930s)
Csepel, Hungary (1950s–60s)
Cushman, USA (1930s–65)
Custer, USA (1936–44)
Cycle-Scoot, USA (1953–55)
CZ, Czechoslovakia (1946–late 60s)

Dayton, GB (1955–60)
Delius, West Germany (1949–53)
Derbi, Spain (1953–57)
Derny, France (1952–54)
DKR, GB (1957–66)
DKW, West Germany (1920s–late 50s)
DMW, GB (1957–67)
Doniselli, Italy (early 1950s)
Douglas, (Vespa) (1951–77)
Ducati, Italy (1952–54, 1964–69)
Dunkley, GB (1957–59)
Dürkopp, West Germany (1954–60)

Excelsior, GB (1940s, 1959–62)
Eysink, Holland (1950s)

Faka, West Germany (1953–57)
Fastex, France (1951–52)
FB Mondial, Italy (1950s)
Ferbedo, West Germany (early 1950s)
FM, Italy (early 1950s)
Foldmobile, USA (late 1950s–early 60s)
Frera, Italy (late 1940s)
Frisoni, Italy (early 1950s)
Fuji, Japan (1946–mid-60s)

GAOMA, Italy (mid-1950s)
Garelli, Italy (1959–61)
Giaca, Italy (late 1940s)
Gilera, Italy (1962–66)
Gitan, Italy (1959–60)
Glas, West Germany (1951–56)
Globe, USA (late 1940s–early 50s)
Goggo (*see* Glas)
Göricke, West Germany (1951–56)
Grasshopper, USA (1944)
Griffon/FMC, France (1950s)
Gritzner-Kayser, West Germany (1950s)

Guiller, France (early 1950s)
Guizzo, Italy (early 1960s)

Hap Alzina, USA/West Germany (late
    1950s–early 60s)
Harley-Davidson, USA (1959–65)
Harper, GB (1954–57)
Heinkel, West Germany (1953–65)
Hercules, West Germany (1955–60, late 60s)
Hirano, Japan (late 1950s–early 60s)
Hoffman (Vespa), West Germany (1949–55)
Honda, Japan (1954–64)
Horex, West Germany (1956)
Hummel, West Germany (1952–55)
Husqvarna, Sweden (mid–late 1950s)

IFA (*see* MZ)
Indian, USA (1949–52)
Innocenti, Italy (1945 onwards)
ISO, Italy (1948–60)
IWL, East Germany (1960s onwards)

James, GB (1960–66)
Jawa, Czechoslovakia (1950s–60s)
J. B. Volks Scooter, USA/West Germany
    (early 1960s)
Joe Be, USA/West Germany (late 1950s)

Kingsbury, GB (1919–23)
Kleinschnittger, West Germany (mid-1950s)
Kreidler, West Germany (1953–57)
Kroboth, West Germany (1951–55)

Lambretta (*see* Innocenti)
La Ray, USA (late 1930s)
Laverda, Italy (1959–63)
Lefol, France (1954–55)
Le Jay, USA (1939)
Lenobile, Belgium (1952–54)
Levante, West Germany (early 1950s)
Liberia, France (1951–52)
Lohner, Austria (1951–58)
Lowther, USA (late 1940s)
Lutz, West Germany (1949–54)

Magnat-Debon (*see* Terrot)
Maico, West Germany (1951–66)
Mako, Switzerland (1953)
Malaguti, Italy (1950s–60s)
Mammut, West Germany (1954)
Manurhin, France (1957–61)
Martin-Moulet, France (1950s)
MBM, Italy (early 1960s)
Mead Cycle, USA (late 1930s–50)
Meister, West Germany (mid-1950s)
Mercury, GB (1956–58)
Messerschmitt (Vespa), West Germany
    (1955–mid-60s)
Midget Motors, USA (early 1960s)
Minerva-Van Hauwaert, Belgium (mid-
    1950s)
Minneapolis, USA (late 1950s)
Mitsubishi, Japan (1948–60s)
Monarch, Sweden (1957–60s)
Monet-Goyen, France (1919–25, 1953–late
    50s)
Montesa, Spain (1959–60, 1962–65)
Mors, France (1951–60s)
Mota, West Germany (1955)
Moto Guzzi, Italy (1950–64)
Motobecane/Motoconfort, France
    (1951–late 50s)
Motobi, Italy (1956–mid-60s)
Motobic, Spain (1963–65)
Motom, Italy (early 1950s)
Motor-Glide (*see* Salsbury)
Moto-Scoot, USA (1936–early 50s)
Mustang, USA (late 1930s, 1945–65)
MV Agusta, Italy (1949–54, 1960–64)

Neue Amag, Switzerland (early 1950s)
NSU Lambretta, West Germany (1950–56)
NSU, West Germany (1956–61)

OLD, France (1950s)
Orix, Italy (early 1950s)
OSA, Poland (late 1950s–late 60s)
Oscar, GB (1953)

Paglianti, Italy (1959–60)
Pannonia, Hungary (late 1950s, early 1960s)

Panther, GB (1959–63)
Parilla, Italy (1952–61)
Paul Vallée, France (late 1950s, early 1960s)
Peripoli, Italy (1961)
Peugeot, France (1953–57)
Phoenix, GB (1956–64)
Piaggio (Vespa), Italy (1946 onwards)
Piatti, GB (1952–late 50s)
Pigeon (*see* Mitsubishi)
Pirol, West Germany (1951–54)
Powell, USA (1939–72)
P.P. Roussey, France (1952–56)
Prior, GB (late 1950s)
Progress, GB (late 1950s)
Progress, West Germany (1954–60)
Puch, Austria (1952–late 60s)

Rabbit (*see* Fuji)
Raleigh, GB (1960–64)
Ravat, France (early 1950s)
Reynolds Runabout, GB (1919–24)
Riedel, West Germany (1950–51)
Rieju, Spain (late 1950s–early 60s)
Riverside, USA (late 1950s–early 60s)
Rockford, USA (late 1950s–mid-60s)
Rock-Ola, USA (1938–41)
Roe, GB (1920s)
Röhr, West Germany (1952–57)
Ronnay (Ronard), USA (1940s)
Rumi, Italy (1951–62)

Safeticycles, USA (1920s)
Salsbury, USA (1935–49)
San Cristoforo, Italy (1949–mid-50s)
Sanko Kogyo, Japan (1950s)
Saroléa, Belgium (late 1950s)
Scootamota (*see* ABC Scootamota)
Scootavia, France (1952–54)
Servetta, Spain (*see* Innocenti)
Servos, West Germany (1953–54)
Showa, Japan (late 1950s)
Sicraf, France (1951–52)
SIM, Italy (1951–56)
Simplex, USA (late 1950s–early 60s)

Simson, East Germany (1955–mid-60s)
Speedway, USA (1945–late 40s)
Sport, France (1950)
Sportcycle, USA (1930s)
Sterling, France (1950s)
Strolch, West Germany (*see* Progress)
Sun, GB (1957–60)
Swallow, GB (1946–51)
Swallow, Japan (1955–early 60s)

Terrot, France (1951–late 50s)
Till (*see* Riedel)
Tote Gate, USA (early 1960s)
Tramnitz, West Germany (1951)
Triumph, GB (1958–70)
Triumph, West Germany (1956–58)
Trojan (Trobike), GB (1960–mid-60s)
Troll, East Germany (1960s onwards)
Trotwood, USA (late 1930s–early 40s)
Tula, Soviet Union (1957 onwards)
TWN (*see* Triumph)

Unibus, GB (1920–22)
URMW, Romania (1957–60)

Vallée (*see* Sicraf)
Varel, West Germany (1951–mid-50s)
Velocette, GB (1960–late 60s)
Venus, West Germany (1953–55)
Victoria, West Germany (1955–57)
Vittoria, Italy (early 1950s)
Vjatka, Soviet Union (late 1950s)
Volugrafo, Italy (1940s)

Wabo, Holland (1950s)
Walba, West Germany (1949–early 50s)
Welbike (*see* Excelsior)
WFM (OSA), Poland (1957–1963)
Whippet, GB (1920–21)

Yamaha, Japan (1960)

Zanella, Argentina (1959–63)
Zündapp, West Germany (1951 onwards)

Note: Manufacturing dates refer to scooter production only.

# INDEX